Islamic 'Aqidah and Fiqh

A Textbook of Islamic Belief and Jurisprudence

Revised and Expanded Edition of
Tawhid & Fiqh

B. Aisha Lemu

Junior Level • General

IQRA' International Educational Foundation
Chicago

Part of a Comprehensive and Systematic Program of Islamic Studies

Program of Aqidah & Fiqh
Junior Level / General

Islamic ‘Aqidah and Fiqh

Chief Program Editors
Dr. Abidullah al-Ansari Ghazi
(Ph.D., History of Religion
Harvard University)

Tasneema Khatoon Ghazi
(Ph.D., Curriculum-Reading
University of Minnesota)

Religious Review and Revision
Maulana Shu‘aib ud-Din Qutub
(Fāḍil Dar ul-Ulum, Karachi)

Maulana Obaidullah Saleem
(Fāḍil Dar ul-Ulum, Deoband)

Language Editing
Hina Naseem Akhtar
(B.S. University of Maryland)

Huda Quraishi-Ahmed
(B.S./B.A., University of Illinois, Chicago)

English Typesetting
Shaista N. Ali
(M.A. Mass Communications, Karachi
University, Pakistan)

Cover Design & Production
Kathryn Heimberger
(A.A.S. American Academy of Art)

Fifth Printing June, 2007
Proudly Printed in the U.S.A

Library of Congress Catalog Card Number 96-79297
ISBN # 1-56316-061-7

TABLE OF CONTENTS

I. ISLĀMIC AQĪDAH

II. FIQH

The cost of printing this book was made possible through a donation from the family of the late Tāhīr Jalil Kidwai with the intention of *Isal Ath-Thawab* (إيصال الثواب) on her soul, so please remember her in your *Du'a'*.

Acknowledgments

I would like to thank my husband, Sheikh Ahmed Lemu, Grand *Qādī* of the *Shari`ah* Court of Appeal, Niger State, for checking the manuscripts and offering much useful advice.

B. Aisha Lemu, Islāmic Foundation, Mina
December 1996

Preface of the Author

I am very grateful to IQRA' International Educational Foundation for publishing *Islāmic Aqīdah and Fiqh,* the revised edition of my textbook, *Tawḥid and Fiqh,* for the junior level and incorporating it into the IQRA' Comprehensive Program for Islamic Education.

During the eighties, when I first devised the Program of Islamic Studies for Nigerian schools, I proposed a new approach to the teaching and presentation of Islāmic Studies in response to the challenge of modern ideologies and the information revolution. Mere memorization of beliefs and rituals without a rational explanation of their significance was fast losing its validity as a method of learning. I am grateful to Allāh ﷻ for making this approach popular not only in Nigeria and West Africa but across the world.

This textbook was originally written according to the *Māliki Fiqh* in accordance with the needs of the Nigerian syllabi at the time of publication. It also covers additional topics that every young Muslim should know. The textbook became very popular after its first printing and was published in several authorized and unauthorized editions. IQRA's revised edition offers a broadened perspective by including the views of all the schools of *Fiqh.* In addition, the overall quality of production has been vastly improved.

As Muslims we know that the Qur'ān is full of rational argument. In fact, it is this quality that gives its message its irrefutable power, thereby bringing those who study it to a state of *'Imān.* The Prophet ﷺ put special emphasis on a logical approach to presenting Islam's message to the first generation of Muslims. Therefore, as Muslim educators, we must follow his example and provide the rationale behind the tenets of Islam.

In the modern world, the entire methodology of teaching has been revolutionized and institutionalized. Therefore, to keep up with the demands of our rapidly changing world, we must apply modern methodology to the writing and teaching of Islāmic Studies. The frustration a Muslim student faces is thus: while going through public school education, he is facilitated by professionally produced textbooks, trained teachers anda proper educational environment, whereas he is faced with a very traditional, often antiquated, approach in his Islāmic education. Islamic education is at a loss in the comparison. Ultimately, it is the student who loses out.

Only if we are able to challenge the spirit and intellect of our youth, will they find the inspiration to become models of Islāmic behavior. If supplied with authentic, well-produced information, a resourceful teacher can create a dynamic learning environment for students of Islāmic Studies that combines mental excitement, communication and interaction.

At the beginning of each volume of this series, some brief notes are given to guide the teacher. However, for detailed discussion of teaching methods, the teacher should refer to my earlier book: *Methodology of Primary Islāmic Studies - a Handbook for Teachers*, published by Islāmic Publication Bureau, P.M.B. 3881, Lagos. Nigeria.

IQRA' NOTE: To Parents and Teachers

IQRA' Foundation is pleased to publish the revised and expanded edition of *Tawhīd and Fiqh* by Hajjah Aisha B. Lemu. This textbook, like its sister volume *Tahdhīb and Sīrah* (now revised and published by IQRA' as *Islāmic Tahdhīb and Akhlāq: In Theory and Practice*) was originally published in 1983 for the junior high school curriculum of Nigerian schools. It covered the *Māliki Fiqh,* which is the most prevalent school of jurisprudence in Nigeria and West Africa. It was later published and used in Islamic schools throughout the U.K. and the U.S. The textbook has been fully revised to cover four other schools of *Sunnī Fiqh* and reviewed by several scholars to ensure authenticity.

Teaching Islamic *Aqā'id* and *Fiqh* has been a serious challenge for Islamic schools in Western societies. All the schools of Islamic *Fiqh* are practiced by a diverse population of Muslims attending the same schools and belonging to the same mosques. The Muslim world has long been divided between the followers of the four prominent schools of *Sunnī Fiqh* and the two equally well-known schools of *Shī'ī Fiqh.* Accepting the validity of all schools, Muslims have traditionally been tolerant of those following schools other than their own. All Muslims are advised to follow the *Imām* or community practice wherever there are differences.

However, in a small portion of the population, there have been some conflicts of opinion between the followers of *Shī'ī* and *Sunnī Fiqh.* In reality, however, the actual difference between *Shī'ī* and *Sunnī Fiqh* is no more discernable than the differences among the other schools of *Sunnī Fiqh.* Notably, in most cases, the friction between *Shī'ī* and *Sunnī groups* has had its roots in politics rather than disagreements over issues of *Fiqh.*

Many prominent leaders of *Shī'ī* and *Sunnī* schools have taken steps to bridge this gap and establish accord among all believers. Apart from the long standing *Shī'ī* and *Sunnī Fiqh* controversy, among some *Sunnī* followers, their is a strong loyalty to their own school of *Fiqh.* While the vast majority of Muslims recognize the validity of all the schools of *Fiqh,* friction still tends to arise over certain sensitive issues. Islamic scholars have characterized the differences in *Fiqh* as a *Raḥmah* (Mercy) and not *Zaḥmah* (Hardship) from Allāh ﷻ, much less a factor to divide the *Ummah* and lead it to strife.

Thus far, the North American Muslim community has remained relatively untouched by such dissension. Here, we find Muslim children belonging to all the schools of *Fiqh* (of both *Sunnī* and *Shī'ī* schools) studying together. There is no standard curriculum advocating the superiority of any particular school of *Fiqh*. However, with the growth of the community and immigration of Muslims from all over the world, regional differences may be imported, and schisms may develop, if a serious effort is not made to develop tolerance and basic understanding.

From the very beginning of its efforts, IQRA' International faced the special challenge of developing a program of Islāmic *Fiqh* which addresses the issues relevant to all Muslims. In America, we have all schools of *Fiqh* and sects of Muslims in one school, so it is important that we teach all schools of *Fiqh* without being dogmatic about any of them. Students should be made to understand that the different schools of thought are a *Raḥmah* in our religion, and one's preference of one school is not a reason for division and hostility.

In theory, being tolerant and reasonable seems simple enough. However, when it comes to structuring our educational programs, we still face formidable problems in developing curricula and writing textbooks. Unfortunately, there are no easy solutions.

IQRA' Foundation, in the development of its literature, strongly advocates the unity of the *Ummah*. In hopes of maintaining a positive relationship with the rest of the humanity, the Foundation has striven hard to make of IQRA' literature free of polemics, bias and controversy. At the elementary level, we offered the textbook, Our Faith and Worship Part I and II, primarily in accordance with the *Ḥanafī Fiqh*, but accommodating others as far as possible. At the junior level, we are presenting this textbook, originally written according the *Māliki Fiqh*, accommodating other schools of *Sunnī Fiqh. We have intentionally not included Ja`farī* and *Zaidī Fiqh* for two reasons: (1) It would make the subject range of the book unmanageable and; (2) We need the consensus of *Sunnī* and *Shī'ī* scholars for such an effort. However, in classrooms consisting of *Shī'ī* students, the teachers may use other books of *Fiqh* reflecting the views of *Shī'ī* schools.

We are fully aware of the fact that we cannot discuss all the *Fiqh* issues at this level.

Therefore, those seeking a deeper understanding of their respective schools of *Fiqh* should refer to other books specifically written on their subjects of interest.

We are presenting this revised edition for review and opinion and shall be grateful to receive your opinions and comments. You can help us in improving the content and production by your active participation in the IQRA' Comprehensive Program of Islamic Studies.

Chief Editors
7450 Skokie Boulevard, Skokie, IL. 60077
Tel: 847-673-4072
Fax: 847-673-4095

Jum`ah, 2 Jamādi I 1417
Friday, 5 September 1997

ISLĀMIC AQĪDAH

INTRODUCTORY NOTES ON `AQĪDAH FOR TEACHERS

The aim of this section of the book is to help the student develop a clear understanding for the Islāmic *'Aqīdah* of *Tawḥīd*: the unity of Allāh ﷻ, the guidance of Allāh ﷻ through His prophets and books, His angels, the life after death and accountability on the Day of Judgment.

The teacher should encourage the students to discuss the points raised. He/she should lead them to relate these points to their own experience and perception. They should be able to apply these concepts to other subjects they are learning such as Arts and Crafts, Carpentry, Home Economics (see Lesson 3) and Science (see Lessons 1, 2, 4 and 5). Generating lively discussion should help reinforce the students' beliefs, because it is drawn from the revelation and backed by their own reasoning and observation. They will have learned how to read some of the signs of Allāh ﷻ.

This method will help children face the modern challenges of plurality of ideas and secular materialism, as they are brought up in a world society which is becoming secular and pluralistic.

The text that follows and the exercises at the end of each lesson should not be regarded as mere statements or questions-and-answers, but as discussion points for teachers and students on the way to reaching solid conclusions in important matters.

LESSON 1

WHAT IS ISLĀM, AND WHO IS A MUSLIM?

Islām is submission to Allāh ﷾. Submission means to give oneself physically, emotionally, and spiritually in the service of Allāh ﷾. A Muslim is one who submits to Allāh ﷾. How does a Muslim submit to Allāh ﷾? Basic to a Muslim's belief is the testimony that Allāh ﷾ exists, and that He is One.

أَشْهَدُ أَلاَّ اِلَهِ اِلاَّ اللَّهُ وَحْدَهُ لا شَرِيكَ لَهُ

I bear witness that there is no god besides Allāh, alone, with no partner.

A Muslim also believes that Muḥammad ﷺ is the last messenger of Allāh ﷾.

أَشْهَدُ أَلاَّ اِلَهِ اِلاَّ اللَّهُ وَاَشْهَدُ اَنَّ مُحَمَّدًا عَبْدُهُ وَرَسُوْلُهُ

And I bear witness that Muḥammad is His Servant and Messenger.

This statement of a Muslim's belief is called *Kalimah ash-Shahādah.*

Since we know the above to be true, it follows that the message brought by Prophet Muḥammad ﷺ, the Qur'ān, is Allāh's ﷾ final and perfect guidance for humankind. Therefore, in order to be successful in this life and in the Hereafter, one must study and live by the teachings and lessons of the Qur'ān.

In the Qur'ān, we find prescribed methods of worship and the fundamental laws of life, as Allāh ﷾ intended them. Every aspect of our lives is guided by these basic principles. When we have a question or find ourselves in danger of following the wrong path, we should turn to prayer and guidance of the Qur'ān.

As Muslims, we should learn our role in this life through the example of

Rasūlullāh ﷺ, documented in his words (*Ḥadīth*) and actions (*Sunnah*). In fulfilling this role, we should strive to become a practical examples for our fellow Muslims as well as for all of humanity. If we make a mistake, we should repent at once and try not to repeat our wrong-doing. This is the meaning of submission to Allāh ﷻ.

Thus, we can see that it is not enough for humans to simply believe in Allāh ﷻ and Rasūlullāh ﷺ. Allāh ﷻ wishes us to live in a way that reflects our sincerity in these beliefs.

In this textbook, we shall deal with the beliefs (*Aqā'id*) of a Muslim and what actions he/she is responsible for. The Qur'ān and the *Sunnah* teach us what righteous belief is(*`Aqīdah*) and describe the actions to enhance our belief. Allāh ﷻ tells us that He and our fellow human beings have certain rights over us, and we must consider it our duty to fulfill them. Allāh's ﷻ rights over us are called *`Ibādat*. The rights of our fellow human beings are called *Mu`amalat*. The subject which teaches the details of our duties to Allāh ﷻ is called the *Fiqh*. We shall study these details of the *Fiqh of `Ibādāt* in the second part of this book.

Our other textbook, *Islamic Akhlāq and Tahdhīb : In Theory and Practice,* deals with the details of *Mu`amalat* and correct Islamic behavior with other people.

✔ EXERCISES

1. How can a person find out what kind of behavior Allāh ﷻ likes and dislikes?
2. What is Islām?
3. What is a Muslim?
4. In your best handwriting, write out the *Kalimah ash-Shahādah* in Arabic, and write its meaning in English.
5. What is the definition of *`Ibādat*?
6. What is the definition of *Mu`amalat*?

7. How do we learn the details of *`Ibādat*?
8. What are the sayings and actions of Rasūlullāh ﷺ called?
9. Why is it important to study the meaning of the Qur'ān in addition to memorizing it?

LESSON 2

ISLĀMIC `AQĪDAH: A SUMMARY OF 'ĪMĀN

As Muslims, we are required to have certain beliefs. Every Muslim must believe in the following:

1. *Tawḥīd*: belief in the Unity of Allāh ﷻ, and His Attributes.
2. The angels, as Allāh's creation from light and His servants.
3. The books of Allāh ﷻ: The revelation Allāh ﷻ sent through His messengers.
4 The prophets and messengers of Allāh ﷻ: His chosen people through whom He sent His messages to humankind.
5. The *Ākhirah*, (the Hereafter): The life after death and the Day of Judgment.
6. The *Qadr*: Allāh's power over His creation.
7. The meaning of Islām and the basic duties of a Muslim.

All of this is a part of a Muslim's *`Aqīdah* (faith) and is called *'Imān* (Belief).

Keep in mind these are only the basic beliefs. They are the foundation of *'Imān*. To be a complete Muslim, you need to know more about Islām. As you study the remaining sections of this book and other books in the Program of Islamic Studies, you will learn more about the actual practices required to live as a true Muslim.

As Muslims, we have a lot to learn. The Qur'ān tells us clearly:

ٱقْرَأْ بِٱسْمِ رَبِّكَ ٱلَّذِى خَلَقَ ﴿١﴾

Read in the name of your Lord Who created you.
(*Al-`Alaq 96*:1)

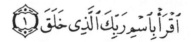

Allāh ﷻ, in His mercy, has provided us with all the information we need. We just have to seek it, learn it, and live by it. The answers we are looking for can be found in the following resources:

1. The message of the Qur'ān, so we can begin to understand Allāh's ﷻ final revelation.
2. The *Sīrah* (biography) of Rasūlullāh ﷺ, so we can learn from his example.
3. The *Aḥādīth*, so that we can understand the words and follow the actions of Rasūlullāh ﷺ.
4. The stories of the prophets ﵈ and some famous Muslims, to learn from the great and noble things they did.
5. *`Aqīdah* and *Fiqh*: so that you may believe in Allāh ﷻ and worship Him in the correct manner and to understand His Laws.
6. Arabic Language, so that we can directly study the Qur'ān and Islamic texts in Arabic and teach them to others.
7. *Akhlāq and Tahdhīb*, so that we may learn the proper Islāmic behavior.

Allāh ﷻ has give us the intelligence to choose between good and evil, and he will reward or punish us according to our belief and actions. Through our efforts, we can become worthy of His love and earn a place in His *Jannah*. He reminds us in the Qur'ān:

وَأَن لَّيْسَ لِلْإِنسَٰنِ إِلَّا مَا سَعَىٰ ﴿٣٩﴾

Verily, for man there is nothing but what he strives for.
(*An-Najm* 53:39)

✓ EXERCISES

1. List and explain the 7 basic beliefs of a Muslim.
2. Is that all a Muslim needs to know?

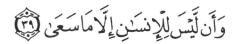

3. Where can a Muslim find the information he needs to lead a truly Islāmic life?
4. Why is the Arabic language important for the study of Islām?
5. What is the difference between *Sīrah* and *Ḥadīth*?

LESSON 3

WHERE DID THE HEAVENS AND EARTH COME FROM?

Have you ever looked at the sky at night? What have you noticed? You may have seen the moon, round like a ball at times, and thin like the tip of a finger nail at others. By observing its changes, we can count the days of the month. You may also have seen thousands of millions of stars in the sky. If you tried to count them all, you could never finish.

Everyday, we see the sun rise in the East and set in the West. With its light, we wake up, we can see the world, and do our work. This same light and warmth causes the plants to grow and the fruits to ripen. Many animals also wake up when the sun rises, and go out to find their food.

Have you ever wondered where the sun, the moon, the stars, and the earth came from? This is an important question. Did anybody make them, or did they make themselves? Does the sun have a brain? Could it have made itself? Could it generate its own energy? Does the moon have a brain? Could it know how to change its shape as the days of the month go by? Does the earth have a brain? Does it know how to make the air, the water, the plants, and the animals?

We know that the sun and the moon, the earth and the stars do not have a brain. They could not make themselves. If they did not make themselves, then who made them? The name of that Maker of the heavens and the earth is Allāh سُبْحَانَهُ وَتَعَالَىٰ.

The Qur'ān says:

تَبَارَكَ ٱلَّذِى جَعَلَ
فِى ٱلسَّمَآءِ بُرُوجًا وَجَعَلَ فِيهَا سِرَٰجًا وَقَمَرًا مُّنِيرًا ﴿٦١﴾

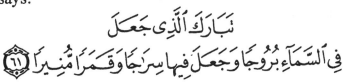

Blessed is He Who made the heaven mansions of the stars,
and placed therein a (radiant) lamp and a moon giving light.
(*Al-Furqān* 25:61)

What caused the world and all the living things to come into existence? Who made the first chicken, the first apple, the first man? Who causes them to stay alive and to reproduce themselves right up until this day?

It is Allāh ﷿, the Creator of the heavens and the earth. In the Qur'ān, He is called *Al-Ḥayy*, The Living One. He is the Giver of life. He is also called *Al-Rabb*, The Sustainer, which means the One Who keeps things alive and provides for all their needs. And so, every day, we pray to Allāh ﷿ by the words of *Sūrah Al-Fātiḥah*:

ٱلْحَمْدُ لِلَّهِ رَبِّ ٱلْعَٰلَمِينَ ۝٢

Praise be to Allāh, the Lord and Sustainer of all the worlds.
(*Sūrah Al-Fātiḥah* 1:2)

We have learned that Allāh ﷿ is the One God, the Creator of all that is in the heavens and the earth. Yet, Allāh ﷿ was not created by anyone or anything. He has always existed and will always exist. One of His Names is *Al-'Awwal, al-Ākhir*, which means "The First and The Last."

Human beings are very intelligent, but they cannot create something out of nothing. The carpenter may say, "I have made a chair." Yet, he cannot make a chair without wood or metal. He can only use what Allāh ﷿ has created. A baker may say, "I have made a cake." But, she cannot make a cake without flour, eggs, butter, and sugar. She cannot create a cake out of nothing.

Only Allāh ﷿ has the power to create out of nothing. Allāh ﷿ has another name in the Qur'ān, *Al-Khāliq*, which means "The Creator." This trait is powerfully established in the following verse of the Qur'ān:

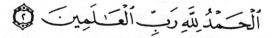

إِنَّمَآ أَمۡرُهُۥٓ إِذَآ أَرَادَ شَيۡـًٔا أَن يَقُولَ لَهُۥ كُن فَيَكُونُ ٨٢

When He wills a thing, He says to it only 'Be!' and it is.
(*Yā Sīn* 36:82)

✓ EXERCISES

1. Who is the Creator of the Heavens and the Earth?
2. Who made living things, and who keeps things alive?
3. Write two words in Arabic describing Allāh ﷻ with their English translations?
4. Test whether you can create something out of nothing: Wish for a cake or a bicycle, and say "Be!" Are you able to create something out of nothing? Try to think of something that a human being can create out of nothing.
5. Look at a doll or toy animal. It has the shape of an animal, but is it life? Can it see? Can it hear? Can it eat? Can it breathe? Can it run?
6. Can anyone give life to that toy? Can you make a toy that is alive? Can a man create a living flower, animal or human being?

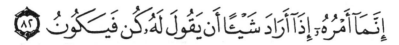

LESSON 4

ALLĀH ﷻ BRINGS THINGS INTO EXISTENCE

Note: *Students should bring as many different kinds of flowers and leaves they can find with them to this lesson.*

In the previous lesson, we learned that only Allāh ﷻ can create something from nothing and give life. Now, let's take a closer look at some of the things that Allāh ﷻ has created. Look at the different flowers and leaves that you brought to class. Are they all the same? You will notice many differences.

1. Compare the **SIZE** of the flowers and leaves.

2. Compare their **SHAPES**. Some are round, some long, some shaped like fans, or knives, or stars, or bells or trumpets.

3. Compare their **COLORS**. How many different colors can you see?

4. Compare their **SMELL**. Some smell sweet, some not very nice, and some have no scent at all.

5. Compare their **TEXTURE**. Some are hard, some soft, some thick and fleshy, some thinner than paper.

Why aren't they all the same? Who has made them different from one another?

Think about some animals you know. You may have seen pictures of other animals in books. If you begin naming them, you will never finish your list, because there are so many. Why are there so many different kinds of animals?

Allāh ﷿ has answered this question in the Qur'ān. He says that He creates what He likes, and that He is never tired of creating. He is called *Al-Bāri', Al-Muṣawwir*, "The Maker and The Fashioner," which means the One Who gives things their shape and their way of being.

Allāh's ﷿ is all-powerful. Think of all the things in the heavens and the earth that were created and given its own unique shape by Him. Who or what can we compare with Allāh ﷿? Indeed, there is nothing that can be compared with Him!

Allāh ﷿ says that even the sun, the moon, the stars and the earth had a beginning, and will one day have an end.

Only Allāh ﷿ has no beginning and no end: He is limitless. Allāh ﷿ is not a created thing, and He is not like the things He created. Allāh ﷿ also has the name *Al-Baqī*, which means "The Everlasting." Everything on earth will die, but Allāh ﷿ exists forever. He says in the Qur'ān:

كُلُّ مَنْ عَلَيْهَا فَانٍ ﴿٢٦﴾ وَيَبْقَىٰ
وَجْهُ رَبِّكَ ذُو الْجَلَٰلِ وَالْإِكْرَامِ ﴿٢٧﴾

All that is on earth will pass away, but will exist forever the face of your Lord, full of Majesty, Bounty and Honor.
(*Ar-Raḥmān* 55:26-7)

✔ EXERCISES

1. Why doesn't Allāh ﷿ need children or family?
2. Why is it useless to worship someone other than Allāh ﷿.
3. Make a list of the different plants and animals you know. How long can each of them live?
4. Is there any creature that lives forever?

LESSON 5

ALLĀH ﷻ IS THE ONLY CREATOR; HE HAS NO PARTNERS

We learned in the previous lesson that Allāh ﷻ was not born, and that He will never die. Since He was not born, He has no father or mother. Since He will not die or grow old, He has no need of children to live after Him or to help Him in old age. Therefore, Allāh ﷻ has no wife, son or daughter. Allāh ﷻ is One, alone and without partner.

Sūrah Al-'Ikhlāṣ teaches us about *Tawḥīd*, the Oneness of Allāh ﷻ:

قُلْ هُوَ ٱللَّهُ أَحَدٌ ﴿١﴾ ٱللَّهُ ٱلصَّمَدُ ﴿٢﴾ لَمْ يَلِدْ
وَلَمْ يُولَدْ ﴿٣﴾ وَلَمْ يَكُن لَّهُۥ كُفُوًا أَحَدٌۢ ﴿٤﴾

Say: He, Allāh, is the One, Allāh, the Everlasting, Allāh, the Eternal.
He does not beget (children), nor is He begotten (by any parents),
And there is nothing that could be compared with Him.
(*Sūrah Al-'Ikhlāṣ* 112:1-4)

Human beings are created by Allāh ﷻ. Some have special talents and gifts from Allāh ﷻ, but no human is perfect. All humans are born, and they all die. They all need to eat, drink and sleep for survival. Only Allāh ﷻ is perfect, and needs nothing to exist.

Allāh ﷻ is not a human being and has no need for any of these things. We should never say that any human being is Allāh ﷻ, or a son of Allāh ﷻ. No human can be a partner of Allāh ﷻ. Allāh is the creator of all and He is not created by anyone.

We should not believe that any human being is a god. It is wrong to worship any of the following:

(a) creatures such as angels or animals;
(b) created objects such as trees, stones, or mountains;
(c) man-made objects such as idols, statues, or pictures;
(d) imaginary gods and spirits.

Worship in Islām is reserved for Allāh ﷻ alone, He is our Lord and Creator. This is the pure faith taught by all the prophets عليهم السلام

In every prayer, we use the words of *Sūrah Al-Fātiḥah*:

إِيَّاكَ نَعْبُدُ وَإِيَّاكَ نَسْتَعِينُ ٥

You (Allāh ﷻ) alone we worship, and You alone we ask for help.
(*Sūrah Al-Fātiḥah* 1:5)

All of us come from Allāh ﷻ and one day, we will return to him. Life is our journey back to our Creator. We begin this journey as babies, helpless and dependent on our parents to take care of us and love us. They teach us the difference between right and wrong, and the ways of the world. As we grow older, our experience of the world makes us wiser, and soon, we can take care of ourselves. As adults, we are strong, independent, and often feel like nothing can hurt us. Eventually, our bodies become weak, and our health often makes us dependent on others once again, almost helpless, like we were when we were babies. As we grow older, we get closer to the end of our time on earth. However, life and death is decided by Allāh ﷻ alone, and anyone's death can come at anytime.

Allāh ﷻ tells us in Qur'ān that we were put on this earth to worship Him alone and then to return to Him.

That is why, when anyone dies, we say:

إِنَّا لِلَّهِ وَإِنَّا إِلَيْهِ رَاجِعُونَ ١٥٦

Indeed, we belong to Allāh, and indeed to Him, we shall return.
(*Al-Baqarah* 2:156)

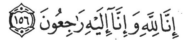

So, we must always be ready to meet our Maker. We must do good deeds and win His favor to be included in those who will enter Paradise.

✔ EXERCISES

1. Why doesn't Allāh ﷻ need parents or children?
2. Can a human being be God?
3. Name some of the things a Muslim should not worship, and discuss why it is useless to worship them.
4. Where will we go when we die?

LESSON 6

THE SIGNS OF ALLĀH ﷻ

The signs of Allāh's existence are evident in every aspect of our lives. Because these signs are so numerous, they are sometimes easy to take for granted. According to the Qur'ān, every Muslim should seek out these signs. We should look around us and reflect upon the creation and its purpose. Increasing our awareness in such a manner strengthens our '*Imān* and brings us closer to the Creator, Allāh ﷻ. Here is a very important passage from the Qur'ān about the signs of Allāh ﷻ for students to study:

وَإِلَٰهُكُمْ إِلَٰهٌ وَٰحِدٌ ۖ لَّآ إِلَٰهَ إِلَّا هُوَ ٱلرَّحْمَٰنُ ٱلرَّحِيمُ ﴿١٦٣﴾
إِنَّ فِى خَلْقِ ٱلسَّمَٰوَٰتِ وَٱلْأَرْضِ وَٱخْتِلَٰفِ ٱلَّيْلِ وَٱلنَّهَارِ
وَٱلْفُلْكِ ٱلَّتِى تَجْرِى فِى ٱلْبَحْرِ بِمَا يَنفَعُ ٱلنَّاسَ وَمَآ أَنزَلَ ٱللَّهُ
مِنَ ٱلسَّمَآءِ مِن مَّآءٍ فَأَحْيَا بِهِ ٱلْأَرْضَ بَعْدَ مَوْتِهَا وَبَثَّ فِيهَا
مِن كُلِّ دَآبَّةٍ وَتَصْرِيفِ ٱلرِّيَٰحِ وَٱلسَّحَابِ ٱلْمُسَخَّرِ
بَيْنَ ٱلسَّمَآءِ وَٱلْأَرْضِ لَءَايَٰتٍ لِّقَوْمٍ يَعْقِلُونَ ﴿١٦٤﴾

And your god is One God: there is no god but Him, the Most Gracious, the Merciful.Truly, in the creation of the heavens and the earth and the difference of night and day; and the ships that run upon the sea with that which is useful to man; and in the waters which Allāh sends down from the sky; thereby reviving the earth after it had been lifeless; and causing all manner of living creatures to multiply thereon; and in the change of the winds; and the clouds that run their appointed courses between the sky and the earth: (in all this) there are signs for people who use their reason.

(*Al-Baqarah* 2: 163-164)

In examining these signs of Allāh ﷻ, we can better understand the different schemes of life. We understand the answers to complex questions, such as:

1. Who could be great enough to create the magnificent stars in the sky, and also the tiny grains of pollen on a flower?

2. Who could be mighty enough to create the earth with its mountains, rivers and seas?

3. What causes heavy ships to float on water? If you place an iron nail in the water, it will sink. But if you put a great iron ship in the water, it will stay afloat. Why?

4. Clouds are made of water. Water is heavier than air. How does so much water get up into the sky? And why doesn't it fall all at once?

5. What causes water to bring seeds to life? Why does the earth have so much water? Two-thirds of the earth is covered by water (the sea). What is the wisdom in that?

6. Why are there so many different kinds of animals and plants? What gives them their individual characteristics?

7. What causes the winds to change? Why don't they always blow in the same direction around the world?

8. What causes the clouds to be carried here and there by the winds, coming and going between the different seasons?

Some may say that all of these things happen as a result of nature. The question arises: "What is nature?" The word "nature" is used to describe certain basic behavior. For example, the nature of an ant is to live in a nest. The nature of a bee is to make honey. The nature of a bird is to fly and sing. By the Islāmic definition, "nature" characterizes the Signs of Allāh ﷻ. We praise Him for all His signs, which we see in the world around us, by saying:

بِسْمِ ٱللَّهِ ٱلرَّحْمَٰنِ ٱلرَّحِيمِ ﴿١﴾

ٱلْحَمْدُ لِلَّهِ رَبِّ ٱلْعَٰلَمِينَ ﴿٢﴾

In the name of Allāh, the Most Gracious, the Merciful.
Praise be to Allāh, the Lord and Sustainer of all the worlds.
(*Al-Fātiḥah* 1:1-2)

When you study geography and science, you can learn a lot about how these things work. The more you know about how they work, the more you will marvel at Allāh's arrangement, power and wisdom. Despite all the knowledge that science, geography, and other disciplines provide mankind, there is a wealth of knowledge that remains untapped, only to be known by Allāh ﷾. This is what scientists refer to as the "mysteries of life." Perhaps, Allāh ﷾ may choose to unravel these mysteries some day. Until then, we must continue our search for His Signs and try to gain wisdom in what He has provided us.

✔ EXERCISES

1. What is the use of looking at the heavens and the earth and thinking about them?
2. Did "nature" create the heavens and the earth?
3. What is "nature" in the Islamic context?

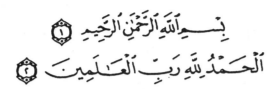

LESSON 7

THE NAMES OF ALLĀH ﷻ

In all that we have said about Allāh ﷻ, we can see that He has many names (attributes). Through His names, we learn of His powers and His traits. This information is useful in learning how to better serve Him. You may have heard of the ninety-nine "Beautiful Names of Allāh ﷻ." They are found in different parts of the Qur'ān. You have already learned some of them.

There is one particular passage in the Qur'ān in which Allāh ﷻ reveals much about Himself through many of His names and attributes:

هُوَ ٱللَّهُ ٱلَّذِى لَآ إِلَٰهَ إِلَّا هُوَ ۖ عَٰلِمُ ٱلْغَيْبِ وَٱلشَّهَٰدَةِ ۖ
هُوَ ٱلرَّحْمَٰنُ ٱلرَّحِيمُ ﴿٢٢﴾ هُوَ ٱللَّهُ ٱلَّذِى لَآ إِلَٰهَ إِلَّا هُوَ
ٱلْمَلِكُ ٱلْقُدُّوسُ ٱلسَّلَٰمُ ٱلْمُؤْمِنُ ٱلْمُهَيْمِنُ ٱلْعَزِيزُ
ٱلْجَبَّارُ ٱلْمُتَكَبِّرُ ۚ سُبْحَٰنَ ٱللَّهِ عَمَّا يُشْرِكُونَ
﴿٢٣﴾ هُوَ ٱللَّهُ ٱلْخَٰلِقُ ٱلْبَارِئُ ٱلْمُصَوِّرُ ۖ لَهُ ٱلْأَسْمَآءُ ٱلْحُسْنَىٰ ۚ
يُسَبِّحُ لَهُۥ مَا فِى ٱلسَّمَٰوَٰتِ وَٱلْأَرْضِ ۖ وَهُوَ ٱلْعَزِيزُ ٱلْحَكِيمُ ﴿٢٤﴾

Allāh is He, besides Whom there is no other god: The Knower of the visible and the invisible; He is the Most Gracious, Most Merciful. Allāh is He, besides Whom there is no other god: the King, the Holy, the Source of Peace and Salvation, the Keeper of Faith, the Guardian, the Majestic, the Compeller, The Supreme! Glory to Allāh ! High is He above the partners that (men) may attribute to Him. He is Allāh , the Creator, The Shaper out of naught. His (alone) are the Most Beautiful Names; All that is in the

heavens and the earth glorify Him and He is the Mighty, the Wise!
(*Al-Ḥashr* 59: 22-24)

Two very important names of Allāh, found in the Qur'ān repeatedly, and at the beginning of almost every *Sūrah*, are *Ar-Raḥmān, Ar-Raḥīm*, "The Most Gracious, the Most Merciful." From these names, we understand the magnitude of Allāh's Grace and Mercy. We find evidence of this fact in every blessing He has given us. Think about what Allāh has done for you: it is overwhelming. We should remember Allāh's blessings to us and be grateful for His Mercy.

In another verse, Allāh says:

ٱللَّهُ نُورُ ٱلسَّمَٰوَٰتِ وَٱلۡأَرۡضِۚ

Allāh is the Light of the Heavens and the earth.
(*An-Nūr* 24:35)

Allāh also says in the Qur'ān:

وَنَحۡنُ أَقۡرَبُ إِلَيۡهِ مِنۡ حَبۡلِ ٱلۡوَرِيدِ ١٦

And We (God) are nearer to him (man) than his jugular vein.
(*Qāf* 50:16)

We know that Allāh is so great, because He is never far away, where He cannot see or hear us. He says:

وَقَالَ رَبُّكُمُ ٱدۡعُونِيٓ أَسۡتَجِبۡ لَكُمۡ

Call unto Me and I will respond to you.
(*Ghāfir* 40:60)

Moreover, it has been reported by Abu Hurairah that Rasūlullāh said:

Iḥsān is to worship Allāh as if you see Him; and if you do not achieve this state of devotion, then Allāh sees you.
(Transmitted by Muslim)

Obviously, it is important that we are conscious of Allāh ﷻ at all times, and that we behave with the full understanding that He is present with us and a Witness to all that we do.

✔ EXERCISES

1. Discuss the meaning of the above passage of the Qur'ān (*Sūrah Al-Ḥashr* 59, verses 22-24).
2. Memorize the passage in Arabic.
3. Memorize the meaning of the passage in English.
4. Write out the passage in your best handwriting in Arabic and in English.
5. In what ways is Allāh ﷻ Gracious and Merciful to human beings?
6. What are some of the things that you like best in this world, which Allāh ﷻ has provided for you?

LESSON 8

CREATION OF THE FIRST MAN

Allāh ﷻ describes in the Qur'ān how He created the first man, Ādam ؑ, out of clay, and gave him human qualities. Finally, as His greatest gift, Allāh ﷻ breathed life into him.

Allāh ﷻ blessed Ādam ؑ with the gift of speech and the ability to communicate with other beings. Ādam ؑ was also given intelligence, emotions, and the ability to reason. He was blessed with the freedom of choice to obey or to disobey His commands. Man is truly a unique creation.

Allāh ﷻ ordered the angels to respectfully bow down to Ādam ؑ. Since they were created to obey Allāh's commands unquestioningly, the angels obeyed. However, among them was a stubborn *jinn*, named Iblīs. He refused to bow to Ādam ؑ, protesting:

قَالَ أَنَا۠ خَيْرٌ مِّنْهُ خَلَقْتَنِى مِن نَّارٍ وَخَلَقْتَهُۥ مِن طِينٍ ﴿٧٦﴾

I am better than he is; You have created me out of fire, whereas You have created him out of clay.
(*Ṣād* 38:76)

Allāh ﷻ created the *Jinn* before He created human beings. They are created from fire. Like humans, they have the freedom to obey or disobey Allāh ﷻ. Therefore, some *Jinn* are good, and others are bad. On the Day of Judgment, they too will be judged for their actions.

Iblīs was proud and rebelled against Allāh ﷻ. Allāh ﷻ cursed him and could have destroyed him that very instant, but Shaiṭān (another name for Iblīs) begged Allāh ﷻ to delay his punishment until the Day of Judgment. Allāh ﷻ, in His infinite wisdom, decided to grant his request to teach him a lesson.

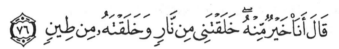

The ungrateful Shaiṭān vowed to lead Ādam عليه السلام and all other human beings astray. Allāh سبحانه وتعالى gave him permission to try, but told the Shaiṭān that His true servants would never be led astray. Allāh سبحانه وتعالى also warned him that, on the Day of Judgement, He would condemn the Shaiṭān and those who followed him to Hell for a torturous eternity. Thus was the beginning of Allāh's test to all human beings until the Day of Judgement.

How does the Shaiṭān lead people astray? He tries many ways to deceive people, whispering in their minds, confusing bad with good. Some human beings behave like Shaiṭān by misleading others into wrong-doing, creating false justification for evil ideas. They are called "the Shaiṭān of men."

How can we avoid following Shaiṭān into doing wrong? First, we should study the teachings of Allāh سبحانه وتعالى thoroughly, so we can recognize good from bad, and right from wrong. The better informed we are, the stronger our *'Īmān* will become. Armed with knowledge and the truth, the Shaiṭān's attempts to deceive us will fail.

Second, we should always try to worship Allāh سبحانه وتعالى with complete devotion, even if this sometimes becomes difficult. This is the only way we can gain Allāh's protection and guidance in our struggle against Shaiṭān. We must always remember that we should prepare for the Day of Judgement, and that our every deed is being recorded.

Third, when we are tempted to do something wrong, we should seek guidance in Allāh سبحانه وتعالى:

أَعُوذُ بِاللهِ مِنَ الشَّيْطَانِ الرَّجِيْمِ

I seek refuge in Allāh from the accursed Shaiṭān.

It is not enough just to say it: we must be firm and take action to get away from evil. A great Muslim scholar, Imām Al-Ghazāli, wrote that a person who simply recites the above *du'ā'*, but fails to make an effort to get away from evil, is like a man who sees a lion coming to attack him, but simply states: "I seek refuge in that tree over there," without making any move to run towards the tree.

Thus, we must make a genuine effort to avoid evil actions, and pray to Allāh ﷻ to help us in this effort. Allāh ﷻ has given us a *Sūrah* in the Qur'ān for such circumstances. In this *du'ā'*, we ask Allāh ﷻ to protect us from any kind of Shaiṭān who may whisper into our minds:

قُلْ أَعُوذُ بِرَبِّ ٱلنَّاسِ ﴿١﴾ مَلِكِ ٱلنَّاسِ ﴿٢﴾ إِلَٰهِ
ٱلنَّاسِ ﴿٣﴾ مِن شَرِّ ٱلْوَسْوَاسِ ٱلْخَنَّاسِ ﴿٤﴾ ٱلَّذِى
يُوَسْوِسُ فِى صُدُورِ ٱلنَّاسِ ﴿٥﴾
مِنَ ٱلْجِنَّةِ وَٱلنَّاسِ ﴿٦﴾

Say: I seek refuge with the Lord of men, the King of men, the God of men. From the evil of the whispering tempter, who whispers into the hearts of men from among jinn and among men.
(*An-Nās* 114:1-6)

✔ EXERCISES

1. How did Allāh ﷻ make Ādam ؑ?
2. What did Allāh ﷻ teach Ādam ؑ?
3. Why did Shaiṭān refuse to bow to Ādam ؑ?
4. What did Shaiṭān say he would do to men?
5. How does Shaiṭān lead people astray?
6. What should a person do to avoid being led astray?

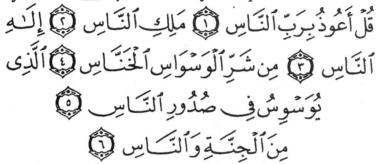

LESSON 9

ALLĀH ﷻ, THE GUIDE

We have learned that we were created to worship Allāh ﷻ. He has placed us on this earth to test whether we will obey Him or not. As tools for this test, He has given us intelligence to recognize good from bad. In addition, He has given us guidance in the form of instincts that guide our conscience. Allāh ﷻ has also provided us with the guidance of the Qur'ān and the example of His Prophet ﷺ to show us how to use our instincts and intelligence. His angels serve to carry out his orders and help us in ways we don't know and can't see. Truly, He has given us every chance for success in this test.

Allāh ﷻ has given us the ability to look after ourselves. Similarly, He created animals with special survival instincts. An instinct is a form of guidance inside every living thing. Who teaches a duckling how to swim? Who teaches a little bird how to fly? Who teaches a baby to drink milk? All of these instincts necessary for survival are present at birth. Remarkably, no one taught them these inborn behaviors. A scientist may call this phenomenon "nature," but as Muslims, we know that Allāh ﷻ has created every creature certain innate characteristics that enable it to survive and grow.

Allāh ﷻ also gave us special guidance through His prophets ﷺ. Their mission was to teach their people to use their intelligence and wisdom in the service of Allāh ﷻ. The prophets ﷺ defined good and bad behavior, as Allāh ﷻ revealed it to them. Their lives are examples that we must follow.

Prophet Muḥammad ﷺ is called *Khātim an-Nabiyyīn*, "the Seal of the Prophets." We know that he is the final prophet *(Al-Aḥzāb* 33:40). No other prophet or messenger will come after him. His message is a complete one; one that will last forever. This complete and final guidance to all mankind is the Qur'ān. In it, we find answers to all the questions of life. If we study the Qur'ān with open minds and hearts, we are bound to find the keys to success in this life and in the Hereafter. As stated in the Qur'ān, we are blessed that Allāh ﷾ is *Al-Hādī*, "The Guide."

✔ EXERCISES

1. Who gives the animals their instinct to stay alive?
2. How does Allāh ﷾ guide human understanding?
3. Why does Allāh ﷾ know best how to guide man?
4. What should a person do to be happy in this world and the next?
5. If you want to find out how to please Allāh ﷾, where would you look for guidance?

LESSON 10

MALĀI'KAH: THE ANGELS

The angels were created by Allāh ﷻ as His servants. They are invisible creatures made of divine light (*Nūr*). We cannot see them unless by Allāh's ﷻ permission, but they can see us.

They are created to carry out the commands of Allāh ﷻ. They do not possess the ability to choose right from wrong like we do. They have been created solely to obey Allāh ﷻ. Therefore, they are always good.

They serve Allāh ﷻ in many different ways. Some of them carry Allāh's messages for the guidance of mankind. Others record our deeds. And still others carry out Allāh's commands and regulate natural occurrences, such as rainfall. They encourage and help the believers when they are in difficulty or danger. There are special angels who guard Heaven and Hell.

They have no free will of their own. They have no personal desires and no feelings of hunger and sex. There is no male or female among them. Their knowledge is limited to what Allāh ﷻ has given them.

Some of the angels are assigned special tasks. Some of them are created to glorify Allāh ﷻ. Some of the angels go around the *'Arsh*, the seat of Divine manifestation, and continuously praise Allāh ﷻ. There are angels who are in charge of *Jannah* and they welcome the believers as they enter *Jannah*. There are other angels who are responsible for *Jahannum*, and they wait for the disbelievers to arrive. They ask them: "Why did you not believe when the message of Allāh ﷻ had come to you and many prophets gave you warnings of this coming day?"

Whenever we hear the name of an angel, we must say *'Alai-hi (a)s-Salām*, which means, “may peace be upon him.”

The chief of the angels is Jibrīl (Gabriel) ﵇, who was responsible for bringing the message of Allāh ﷻ to the prophets. He brought Allāh’s ﷻ final message of the Qur’ān to Rasūlullāh ﷺ. He is described in the Qur’ān as “very strong” (*Shadīd al-Quwā*), “trustworthy” (*Al-Amīn*) and “generous messenger” (*Rasūlun Karīm*). Rasūlullāh ﷺ saw him on various occasions. One time, he appeared in human form, and even several *Ṣaḥābah* saw him.

Angel Izrā’il ﵇ is responsible for carrying out the order for death. He approaches people, informing them that their time in this world is over, and then he extricates their souls. Angel Isrāfīl ﵇ will blow the trumpet (*Ṣūr*) before the day of Judgment. Its sound will become so fierce and loud that it will shatter and destroy everything. Then, he shall blow the trumpet a second time to recreate everything, thus marking the commencement of the Day of Judgment. Angel Mīkā’īl (Michael) ﵇ is responsible for the rainfall and supply of provisions.

Two angels, *Kirāman Kātibīn*, are assigned to each individual to record their actions on a scroll. One records the good deeds, and the other records the bad deeds. On the Day of Judgment, their record will be presented before Allāh ﷻ. Those who believed and did good deeds will go to *Jannah,* and those who did not believe and did evil deeds will be condemned to *Jahannum*.

Two angels, Munkir and Nakīr, will visit the dead in the grave soon after the burial. They will ask the three questions: 1. Who is your Lord?; 2. Who is your messenger?; and, 3. What is your religion?

The believers will answer these questions correctly and receive the good news of meeting their Lord on the Day of Judgment. The non-believers will be confused and will not know the answers.

✓ EXERCISES

1. What is the role of the angels?
2. Are they Allāh's ﷻ children? Do they share powers with Him?
3. Who is Angel Jibrīl ؑ, and what are his various titles?
4. Can the angels have their own desires, and can they disobey Allāh's commandments?
5. What questions would Munkir ؑ and Nakīr ؑ ask in the grave?
6. Name three important angels and describe their role?

LESSON 11

THE BOOKS OF ALLĀH

Allāh ﷻ is the Creator of all, and He ultimately cares for all His creation. Human beings are His best creation. He has given them knowledge and granted them freedom to choose between good and evil. They are sent to this world for a short period and are given an opportunity to choose between good and evil. They can choose good and be worthy of Allāh's ﷻ love, or follow evil and earn Allāh's ﷻ anger. They will all be judged on the Day of Judgment for their beliefs and actions.

Allāh ﷻ has created human beings on the *Fiṭrah*, the true nature. The *Fiṭrah* means that true human nature is innocent. There is no concept of "Original Sin" in Islām. Islām does not advocate the Christian idea that because Ādam عليه السلام, the first man and the first prophet, disobeyed Allāh ﷻ by eating the forbidden fruit, all humanity is born in sin.

Human beings face many challenges in this life. They also have many desires and the God-given freedom to follow them. The Shaiṭān is always busy trying to misguide them and make them forget Allāh ﷻ. Many times, people succumb to the Shaiṭān's temptations. Sometimes, their environment is bad, and it corrupts even good people. Humans tend to be forgetful, and they need constant reminders. Thus, human *Fiṭrah* requires constant guidance and reminders to remain steadfast on Allāh's path.

Allāh ﷻ knows the nature of His creatures. Out of His love, and He wants to guide them to the right path. From the time of creation, He sent his prophets and messengers to guide humanity to His path and become worthy of His reward in this world and the Hereafter.

Allāh ﷻ sent many prophets (*Anbiyā'*) and sent His *Waḥī*, the revelation, through Angel Jibrīl عليه السلام. Some of the prophets received the *Waḥī* in the form of a book as a complete code. Such prophets are called the messengers (*Rusūl*). Thus, every messenger is a prophet, but every prophet is not a messenger.

The revelations taught them the truth about Allāh ﷻ, the mission of His prophets and the teachings about leading a righteous life. The revelations clearly laid down what is *Ḥalāl,* or permissible, and what is *Ḥarām*, or forbidden.

The teachings revealed by Allāh ﷻ through His prophets and written down in His Books make up Islām. Islām means submission to Allāh ﷻ. The religion of Islām teaches us to submit our will to the Will of Allāh ﷻ and follow His revelation in all walks of life. Islām has been Allāh's ﷻ chosen religion for humanity for all times and all places, and it was revealed to Prophet Muḥammad ﷺ in its final and complete form.

Allāh ﷻ sent His guidance to every people on earth through his prophets and his messengers with His written word. However, most of those books have either been lost or changed. Some of them have been changed beyond recognition. These books may still have some remains of the original teachings of *Tawḥīd* and guidance for moral life, but there are so many changes made by misguided people that the true message can hardly be recognized.

We do not know the exact number of the books, nor do we know which of the existing religious books and sacred literature is truly divine revelation. Allāh ﷻ mentions only five prophets and the names of the books they received in the Qur'ān:

Prophet Ibrāhīm ؑ received the *Ṣuḥuf.*
Prophet Mūsa ؑ received the *Tawrait* (Torah).
Prophet Da'wūd ؑ received the *Zabūr* (Psalms).
Prophet `Isā ؑ received the *Injīl* (Gospels).
Prophet Muḥammad ﷺ received The Qur'ān.

In the next chapter, we shall discuss the truth and authenticity of these books and the Qur'ān. The Muslims must believe in all the books of Allāh ﷻ which are mentioned in the Qur'ān. Muslims must also respect all other sacred and religious books, although we cannot be certain of how authentic they are. We must neither affirm nor deny their divine origin, but show them our respect.

As far as the truth of these books is concerned, we have the teachings of the Qur'ān as the criteria. The truth, as contained in these books, also came from divine revelations. We must seek the truth wherever it is and accept it. Rasūlullāh ﷺ said:

Wisdom is the lost property of a believer he accepts it wherever he finds it.
(Transmitted by Tirmidhi & Ibn Majah)

Islām also forbids us to ridicule other people and laugh at their beliefs and religious practices. If we have differences, we must make our explanations with kindness and understanding.

✓ EXERCISES

1. Compare and contrast the concepts of *"Fiṭrah"* and "Original Sin"?
2. What happened to the earlier revelations?
3. What books are mentioned in the Qur'ān?
4. Name the prophets who received the Books.
5. Why has Allāh ﷻ sent his revelations to people?
6. How should we treat other books which are not mentioned in the Qur'ān?
7. How should Muslims treat people of other religions?

LESSON 12

AL-QUR'ĀN: THE FINAL REVELATION

The Qur'ān is the final revelation of Allāh ﷻ, sent to Prophet Muḥammad ﷺ through Angel Jibrīl ؑ. Allāh ﷻ has promised to safeguard it forever. He promises in the Qur'ān:

إِنَّا نَحْنُ نَزَّلْنَا ٱلذِّكْرَ وَإِنَّا لَهُۥ لَحَٰفِظُونَ ٩

Indeed, we have revealed this Dhikr
(the Qur'ān), and We will safeguard it.
(*Al-Hijr* 15: 9)

Allāh ﷻ sent many prophets with His guidance and many messengers with His books. However, over time, these messages were either lost or changed. The Qur'ān informed us fourteen hundred years ago that all these books have been changed. Most of the modern scholars are confirming this fact. Many of the original teachings have been lost or intentionally removed from the books. Some teachings have been misinterpreted to give them a different meaning. Some words have been changed to give them totally different meanings, and even new teachings have been added to these divine revelations.

We do not even know the names of most of the revealed books. We have a mention of only four other books in the Qur'ān. The *Ṣuḥuf* of Ibrāhīm have been completely lost, and we have no information about them. *Tawrait* and *Zabūr* now form part of Old Testament. The *Injīl* is part of the New Testament. All of these books have gone through many changes, and the original documents are no longer available.

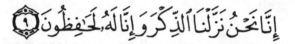

Although these books have been tampered with and distorted, the Qur'ān recognizes them as revealed books and accepts that they still contain some truth. The Qur'ān invited the Jews and Christians to accept the final and complete truth as it was revealed to Rasūlullāh ﷺ. However, if they do not accept the truth of Islām as contained in the Qur'ān, then at least, they are asked to follow the teachings of their revealed books truthfully. The Qur'ān criticizes them for accepting only what suits them and rejecting what is not agreeable to them. It also asked them to read the scriptures, seeking the truth with sincerity instead of trying to find their own ideas within them.

The Qur'ān described the Jews and Christians as *Ahl al-Kitāb,* the People of the Book. Islām established a special relationship between Muslims and the *Ahl al-Kitāb*. Islām also granted them the right to practice their religion freely. The Qur'ān teaches Muslims to speak to them kindly, seek unity with them in the worship of one common God, and cooperate with them in those things that are good and righteous.

There are many other religions, and they have their own sacred books. Although Muslims cannot include other religious groups among the *Ahl al-Kitāb* with certainty, they have traditionally treated them with the same tolerance as they did the Jews and Christians, both socially and politically.

The Qur'ān is Allāh's ﷻ final message. It contains all the truth that had been revealed through the other books, bringing it to a final conclusion. While some of the instructions in earlier books were meant only for a specific time and for a particular people, the message of the Qur'ān is for all times and for all the people. At the time of the earlier prophets, humanity was in its infancy, so Allāh ﷻ did not reveal his complete *Sharī'ah* (Islāmic laws and regulations) then. The Qur'ān completes and finalizes the *Sharī'ah*.

Since the Qur'ān is final revelation, it was important that it be safeguarded from any corruption or change. Allāh ﷻ promised to safeguard it, and we know for a fact that He fulfilled His promise. The Qur'ān is the same book as it was revealed to Prophet Muḥammad ﷺ. As one of the miraculous ways of safeguarding His Word, Allāh ﷻ created love and care about this book in the hearts of the believers, so they would naturally work to preserve it.

There are hundreds and thousands of people all across the world who have memorized the entire Qur'ān word for word. These people are called the *Ḥuffāẓ* (singular: *Ḥāfiẓ*). Every Muslim has some part of the Qur'ān memorized. Some people have learned how to beautifully recite the Qur'ān; they are called *Muqrīs* or *Qārīs*. Yet, there are others who have mastered the art of calligraphy; they write the Qur'ān in an artistic manner. These are called the *Khaṭṭat*. There are scholars who specialize in its study and interpretation. These scholars are called *Mufassirūn* (singular: *Mufassir*).

Generations of Islāmic scholars, known as the *`Ulamā',* have devoted their lives in reading, understanding, practicing and teaching the Qur'ān. The Qur'ān was revealed in the Arabic language, and despite the passing of fourteen hundred years, the Arabic language of the Qur'ān remains a language, spoken, written and understood by the millions. The Qur'ān is not an antiquated book; it was sent as a complete guidance for the *'Ummah* of Prophet Muḥammad ﷺ, and it addresses all the most relevant issues humanity is to face until the end of time.

The Qur'ān gives us a complete code of life. It clearly defines what is *Ḥalāl* and what is *Ḥarām*. It teaches us best morals and manners. There is no part of life that it does not provide us the guidance. This book is for all human beings and for all time to come.

May Allāh ﷻ include us among those who love His book, care about it and strive to safeguard it.

✓ EXERCISES

1. If earlier revelations teach the same truth, why is the Qur'ān needed?
2. In what way have the earlier revelations been changed?
3. Who are the *Ahl al-Kitāb*, and what relationship they have with Muslims?
4. How have the Muslims treated other religious communities?
5. How Allāh ﷻ has safeguarded the Qur'ān.

6. How is the Qur'ān a complete code of life?
7. What are the following people called?
   i. Those who write the Qur'ān.
   ii. Those who recite the Qur'ān.
   iii. Those who interpret the Qur'ān.
   iv. Those who memorize the Qur'ān.

LESSON 13

THE PROPHETS AND MESSENGERS OF ALLĀH ﷻ

Allāh ﷻ says in the Qur'ān:

وَمَا خَلَقْتُ ٱلْجِنَّ وَٱلْإِنسَ إِلَّا لِيَعْبُدُونِ ﴿٥٦﴾

We have not created the Jinns and humans except to worship us.
(*Al-Zāriyāt* 51: 56)

To worship Allāh ﷻ means to believe in *Tawḥīd*; that He is One, and no one is like Him. He is the Creator and Lord of everyone, and no one shares His power. Worshiping Him also means to follow His *Sharī'ah* (Islamic laws, rules and regulations) and lead our lives according to His Will.

How can human beings know what *Tawḥīd* is, and what His Will is? Allāh ﷻ, in His Kindness, has sent many prophets (*Anbiyā'*) and messengers (*Rusūl*) to lead humanity to success in the Hereafter.

A prophet (*Nabī*) is a human being chosen by Allāh ﷻ to receive His message and deliver it to human beings. A prophet is not an angel, *Jinn* or other non-human creature. He is an ordinary human being, a servant of Allāh ﷻ, whom Allāh ﷻ chooses for His Divine purpose.

One cannot choose to be a prophet, it is a gift of Allāh ﷻ that he has given to whomsoever He wishes. A prophet is not required to have any special qualifications, family background or social connections. Only Allāh's ﷻ, decision ordains a particular individual a prophet, and only He knows the reasons for His choice.

Allāh ﷻ sent His prophets to enlighten people all over the world. All of the prophets brought the same message:

- Worship no one but one God.

- Do not commit *Shirk* by accepting partners with Him
- Do not commit *Kufr* by denying His favors to humanity.
- Follow His religion of submission, Islām.
- Lead a moral life according to the divine guidance.
- Prepare yourself for the *'Ākhirah*, you will be judged for his actions committed in this world.

Thus, the message of Allāh ﷻ reached all the people, and Allāh ﷻ left no people or nations without His guidance. Yet, humans have a tendency to become forgetful, and if they are not vigilant, they lose their way. Sometimes, the believers were ruled by evil people who, for their personal interest, changed these pure teachings of Islām. They introduced *Shirk* (hypocrisy) and *Kufr* (disbelief) among the people. They made rules to suit their own needs, instead of adhering to the authentic rules of *Sharī'ah*.

For centuries, Allāh ﷻ kept sending his prophets to lead humanity back to the right path. According to a tradition of the Prophet ﷺ, over one hundred thousand prophets came to this world. We know some of their stories. However, there are many prophets that we know very little about besides their names. And still there were others of whom no record remains (Qur'ān 4:164). There are twenty-five prophets mentioned by name in the Qur'ān: Ādam, Nūḥ, Sāliḥ, Shu'aib, Hūd, Ibrāhīm, Lūṭ, Ismā'īl, Isḥāq, Yā'qūb, Yūsuf, Yūnus, Mūsa, Hārūn, Ayyūb, Dā'ūd, Sulaimān, Ilyās, Al-Yas'ā, Dhul-Kifl, Idrīs, Zakarīyyah, Yaḥya, 'Īsā, and of course, Muḥammad ﷺ

A Muslim must believe and respect all the prophets. The Qur'ān says:

ءَامَنَ ٱلرَّسُولُ بِمَآ أُنزِلَ
إِلَيْهِ مِن رَّبِّهِۦ وَٱلْمُؤْمِنُونَ ۚ كُلٌّ ءَامَنَ بِٱللَّهِ وَمَلَٰٓئِكَتِهِۦ وَكُتُبِهِۦ
وَرُسُلِهِۦ لَا نُفَرِّقُ بَيْنَ أَحَدٍ مِّن رُّسُلِهِۦ ۚ وَقَالُوا۟ سَمِعْنَا
وَأَطَعْنَا ۖ غُفْرَانَكَ رَبَّنَا وَإِلَيْكَ ٱلْمَصِيرُ ﴿٢٨٥﴾

The Messenger believes in what has been revealed to Him from His Lord,

as do the believers. Each one of them believes, in Allāh, and His angels, and His books and His prophets. We make no distinction between one and another of His messengers. And they say we hear and we obey. We seek your forgiveness our Lord, and to you is the end of all journeys.
(*Al-Baqarah* 2: 285)

✓ EXERCISES

1. What are the qualifications to become a prophet?
2. What was the basic message of the prophets?
3. Mention some of the names of important prophets in the Qur'ān.
4. Do Muslims have to believe in all the prophets?
5. What is the difference between a prophet and a messenger?
6. What are the beliefs of the Muslims according to *al-Baqarah* 2:285 ?

LESSON 14

MUḤAMMAD ﷺ: THE LAST MESSENGER

We have learned that Allāh ﷻ has sent many prophets and messengers in the past. All of them taught the message of Islām. Some of them received the books of Allāh ﷻ. However, after some time, the message was lost or corrupted. People started committing *Shirk* and *Kufr*. The prophets came to teach *Tawḥīd*, but their followers started worshiping them as gods, or sons of God, or even incarnations of God.

Finally, Allāh ﷻ decided to send His final prophet and messenger, Muḥammad ﷺ, to all humanity for all times to come. Muḥammad ﷺ was born in Makkah on 12 *Rabī' al-Awwal*, 13 Before *Hijrah* (22 April 571 CE). At the age of forty, Allāh ﷻ chose him as His messenger and gave him the revelation of the Qur'ān. He preached thirteen years in Makkah, but only a few Makkans accepted Islām. After thirteen years, he was invited to migrate (make *Hijrah*) to Madīnah. Most of the people of Madīnah accepted Islām and accepted him as their leader. For ten years, he struggled against the *Kuffār*, the *Munāfiqūn* and the Jews, who opposed and fought against him. Allāh ﷻ gave him a clear victory against His enemies and made Islām victorious.

Prophet Muḥammad ﷺ taught the religion of Islām. It is the same religion which had been taught by all the prophets. The Islām taught by Rasūlullāh ﷺ completes the message brought by all the earlier prophets: Ibrāhīm عليه السلام, Mūsa عليه السلام `Īsa عليه السلام. Allāh ﷻ has promised to preserve the purity of His message and make His *Dīn* (religion) victorious against all other ideologies.

While all the other prophets were sent primarily to their own people, Rasūlullāh ﷺ was sent for all humanity (*Kāffatan li (a)n-Nās*). His message was full of mercy for all the worlds and all the creation, Allāh ﷻ named him *Raḥmatun li (a)l-`Ālamīn*, (a Mercy for all humankind).

Allāh ﷻ gave him the most noble character. He was known as *Al-Amīn* (the Trustworthy) and *Aṣ-Ṣādiq* (the Truthful). Even his enemies recognized the nobility of his life. The Qur'ān says:

وَإِنَّكَ لَعَلَىٰ خُلُقٍ عَظِيمٍ ﴿٤﴾

You (O Muḥammad) are given very high morals and manners.
(*Al-Qalam* 68:4)

Rasūlullāh ﷺ was sent as the best model for all human beings to follow. The Qur'ān says:

لَّقَدْ كَانَ لَكُمْ فِي رَسُولِ ٱللَّهِ أُسْوَةٌ حَسَنَةٌ

Indeed, in the Messenger of Allāh you have a beautiful example.
(*Al-Aḥzāb* 33:21)

He practiced what he preached. *Umm al-mu'minīn* `A'isha̱h said, "His morals were the Qur'ān." Rasūlullāh ﷺ personified in practice everything he taught. His way of life and his teachings are the *Sunnah* (traditions, way) for the *'Ummah* to follow. His teachings, his actions, and the actions that he approved are written and collected in many volumes. The written *Sunnah* is called *Ḥadīth*. *Ḥadīth* means a narration, story or incident. Before he passed away, he said:

I am leaving with you two things, if you will follow them you will never go astray; the book of Allāh and my Sunnah.
(Transmitted by Muslim)

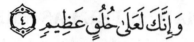

Rasūlullāh ﷺ struggled for the cause of Allāh ﷻ and brought us His message truthfully. He loved his *'Ummah* and asked Allāh's ﷻ forgiveness for its shortcomings. Allāh ﷻ has blessed him with the river *Kawthar* in *Jannah*. Rasūlullāh ﷺ would offer the water of *Kawthar* to his *'Ummah*. Those who shall drink from it shall never go thirsty. On the Day of Judgment, he will be, with Allāh's ﷻ permission, the *Shafī`* (Intercessor) of his *'Ummah*. He will plead to Allāh ﷻ to forgive their sins and admit them to *Jannah.* Allāh ﷻ in His Mercy will accept the *Shafā`ah* of His beloved *Rasūl* and honor his *`Ummah* with the *Jannah.*

Muslims love their prophet. They try to follow His *Sunnah.* They accept what he enjoined and reject what he forbade. The Muslims love his family, *ahl al-Bait,* his *Ṣaḥābah* and respect his wives as their mothers. The Qur'ān says:

ٱلنَّبِيُّ أَوْلَىٰ بِٱلْمُؤْمِنِينَ مِنْ أَنفُسِهِمْ ۖ وَأَزْوَٰجُهُۥٓ أُمَّهَٰتُهُمْ ۗ

The Prophet is closer to the believers than their ownselves,
and his wives are their mothers..
(*Al-Aḥzāb* 33:6)

Allāh ﷻ says about the messenger:

إِنَّ ٱللَّهَ وَمَلَٰٓئِكَتَهُۥ يُصَلُّونَ عَلَى ٱلنَّبِيِّ ۚ يَٰٓأَيُّهَا ٱلَّذِينَ
ءَامَنُوا۟ صَلُّوا۟ عَلَيْهِ وَسَلِّمُوا۟ تَسْلِيمًا ﴿٥٦﴾

Indeed, Allāh and His angels send blessings on the Prophet,
O Believers send blessings on him, and salute him with all respect.
(*Al-Aḥzāb* 33:56)

Whenever we hear the name of Rasūlullāh ﷺ we must say:

صَلَّى اللهُ عَلَيْهِ وَسَلَّمْ

May Allāh's blessings and peace be upon him

✓ EXERCISES

1. Is Islām a new religion? What were the teachings of earlier prophets?
2. What do we mean by the statement: "Muḥammad ﷺ is the final prophet"?

3. What would you call a person who claims to be a prophet or messenger after the coming of Rasūlullāh ﷺ?
4. What is the difference in the mission of Rasūlullāh ﷺ and the other prophets?
5. Why do the believers love Rasūlullāh ﷺ?
6. How does the Qur'ān describe the character and mission of Rasūlullāh ﷺ?
7. What should we say when we hear the name of Rasūlullāh ﷺ.

LESSON 15

THE AKHIRAH: THE HEREAFTER AND WHAT WILL HAPPEN TO US WHEN WE DIE?

Allāh ﷾ tells us in the Qur'ān that He created humans to worship Him. Allāh ﷾ says that He gave men and women life and intelligence to test which of them would obey Him.

Allāh ﷾ has given each human a soul which does not die. When a person dies, his body turns back into earth, but his soul is preserved. On the Day of Judgment, the universe will come to an end, and human beings will be brought back to life. Every one of us will be asked whether we worshiped Allāh ﷾ and behaved righteously on earth.

All the books of Allāh ﷾ teach us that this life is temporary. Eternal life starts after the end of this life. We have been sent here for a very short period of time to be tested for our faith and actions. Allāh ﷾ says:

ٱلَّذِى خَلَقَ ٱلْمَوْتَ وَٱلْحَيَوٰةَ لِيَبْلُوَكُمْ أَيُّكُمْ أَحْسَنُ عَمَلًا ۚ وَهُوَ ٱلْعَزِيزُ ٱلْغَفُورُ ﴿٢﴾

(Allāh) Who has created life and death that he may try you to see which one of you is best in his actions: and He is Mighty and Forgiving.
(*Al-Mulk* 67:2)

The Qur'ān informs us that one day, all life of this world will come to a complete end and it will usher into a new life. Angel Israfil will blow the *Sūr* (the trumpet). As its sound increases, the world will be shattered to pieces. It will be the beginning of the *Qiyāmah,* the Day of Judgment. The Qur'ān gives us many graphic descriptions of that day:

يَوْمَ يَكُونُ ٱلنَّاسُ كَٱلْفَرَاشِ ٱلْمَبْثُوثِ ﴿٤﴾
وَتَكُونُ ٱلْجِبَالُ كَٱلْعِهْنِ ٱلْمَنفُوشِ ﴿٥﴾

A day when humankind will be as scattered moth.
And the mountains will become as carded wool.
(*Al-Qāri`ah* 101:4-5)

This will be the end of all existence. Only Allāh ﷻ would remain that day:

يَوْمَ هُم بَٰرِزُونَ لَا يَخْفَىٰ
عَلَى ٱللَّهِ مِنْهُمْ شَىْءٌ لِّمَنِ ٱلْمُلْكُ ٱلْيَوْمَ لِلَّهِ ٱلْوَٰحِدِ ٱلْقَهَّارِ ﴿١٦﴾

The day they come forth, nothing of them hidden from Allāh.
To whom belongs the Sovereignty and Power this day?
To Allāh the One, Almighty.
(*Al-Mu'min* 40:16)

Then, Allāh ﷻ will ask the Angel Israfīl to blow up the trumpet once more. The second sounding of the trumpet will bring back the creation. People will come out of their graves. That is the Day of *Qiyāmah*, the Judgment. Every soul will be presented before Allāh's seat of power and Majesty. The scrolls of both good and bad deeds prepared by the angels, *Kirāman Kātibīn*, will be presented. Allāh ﷻ would give power of speech to all our organs that day. They will testify before Allāh ﷻ, bringing forth all our good and bad deeds.

The righteous will have the scrolls of their deeds in their right hands, and the evil will have the scrolls of their deeds in their left hands. The faces of the believers will radiate with heavenly light. They receive all that Allāh ﷻ had promised them. The faces of the *Kuffār* will be dark and gloomy. They will be lamenting over their fate and ask Allāh ﷻ to give them a second chance. There will be no second chance that day. They will blame their leaders and

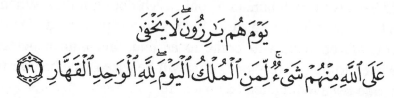

and priests for their ill-guidance. Likewise, the leaders will abandon their people and return the blame upon them.

The believers will have the assurance of the Mercy of Allāh ﷻ and the *Shafā`ah* of Rasūlullāh ﷺ favoring them. They will be admitted to *Jannah.* Their friends, relatives and angels will greet them with, *"Assalāmu `Alaikum"*. Allāh ﷻ Himself would welcome them with *Salām.*

Power, influence, family connections, recommendations of their leaders will do the evil-doers no good that day. Everyone will be judged according to his own deeds. Those who did wrong and did not repent in their lifetime, as well as those who refused to worship and obey Allāh ﷻ will be punished in Hell.

On the Day of Judgment, only Allāh ﷻ will be the judge. No one in this world can say who will be saved, and who will be punished. Allāh ﷻ did not give this authority to any human being. No prophet, priest, magician and leader has the authority to declare another human being as entitled to *Jannah* or the *Jahannum.* However, the Qur'ān and the *Sunnah* have clearly defined the faith and actions that could earn a person access to *Jannah.* It also clearly specifies the evil actions that would lead one to *Jahannum.*

Rasūlullāh ﷺ said:

The actions are determined by the intention.
And everyone gets the reward of what he intends for.
(Transmitted by Bukhārī)

Any action, no matter how good and beneficent, may be rejected by Allāh ﷻ if done with the intent to show off, to earn fame or make worldly profit. While, some seemingly insignificant acts of sincerity may find acceptance with Him.

May Allāh ﷻ reward us with unwavering faith, righteous actions and intentions and raise us with our beloved Rasūlullāh ﷺ and his pious *'Ummah.*

✓ EXERCISES

1. What is the *Qiyāmah*?
2. What actions would help people on the Day of Judgment?
3. How people would come to know about their good or bad deeds?
4. What kind of assurance the believers have on that day?

LESSON 16

WHAT ARE PARADISE AND HELL?

We have learned that on the Day of Judgment, the lives of the human race will be scrutinized and assessed by Allāh ﷻ. All the good and bad they did on earth will be known. Those who did good, and those whom Allāh ﷻ may forgive, will enter Paradise, and the wrong-doers, whom Allāh ﷻ does not forgive, will enter Hell.

What is Paradise? Rasūlullāh ﷺ said that it is beyond anything that we can imagine. Allāh ﷻ has described it in the Qur'ān as a beautiful Garden, in which people will find all the good things that they like best: shady trees, rivers, flowers, beautiful houses and wonderful things to eat and drink, and the company of loved ones. Everything will be a source of peace and happiness; being so close to Allāh ﷻ Himself will be the greatest joy.

What is Hell? It is described in the Qur'ān as a place of fire and heat, or of terrible cold. The people of Hell will be in constant pain. They will blame each other for their condemnation. They will know that their greatest folly was that they rejected Allāh ﷻ, and on that Day, He will reject them.

Here is one of many verses of the Qur'ān that speaks about the Hereafter:

تَرَى ٱلظَّٰلِمِينَ
مُشْفِقِينَ مِمَّا كَسَبُوا۟ وَهُوَ وَاقِعٌۢ بِهِمْ ۗ وَٱلَّذِينَ
ءَامَنُوا۟ وَعَمِلُوا۟ ٱلصَّٰلِحَٰتِ فِى رَوْضَاتِ ٱلْجَنَّاتِ ۖ
لَهُم مَّا يَشَآءُونَ عِندَ رَبِّهِمْ ۚ ذَٰلِكَ هُوَ ٱلْفَضْلُ ٱلْكَبِيرُ ﴿٢٢﴾

You will see the evil-doers fearful of that which they have earned, and it will surely befall them; While those who believed and did good works (will be) in the flowering meadows of the Gardens, having what they wish from their Lord. This is the great preferment.
(*Ash-Shūrā* 42:22)

Which would you rather enter: Paradise or Hell? The people who choose Paradise sincerely believe in Allāh ﷻ and do as much good as they can to win His pleasure. The people destined for Hell earn His anger by disregarding His message and His warnings. May Allāh ﷻ guide us on the right path!

✔ EXERCISES

1. How is Paradise described in the Qur'ān?
2. How is Hell described in the Qur'ān?
3. What should a person do to enter Paradise?
4. How can a person avoid going to Hell?
5. Since it is by doing good deeds that you may enter Paradise, tell your teacher three good deeds which you would like to do or intend to do, *Inshā' Allāh.*

LESSON 17

AL-QADR: THE POWER OF ALLĀH ﷻ
CAN A PERSON CHOOSE TO DO GOOD OR BAD?

Allāh ﷻ has made humans different from animals. Can you think of ways in which we are different from horses, cows, birds, fish, and insects?

Humans are different in several ways. Firstly, humans have intelligence. We have a brain to understand many things. Humans can think and plan. Secondly, humans can speak and put their thoughts and ideas into words. They have the ability to read and write. They can read in books the thoughts of men who lived long ago and far away. Thirdly, every human being has a mind and a heart, allowing him to feel the difference between what is good, and what is bad.

Allāh ﷻ has given us all this intelligence and understanding so that we can recognize Allāh ﷻ as the One Who has created all the wonderful things in the heavens and the earth. He has allowed humans to understand the difference between good and bad. Allāh ﷻ has full power to control all of His creations, including Man. However, He has given us the power to choose between good and bad.

Suppose a mother asks her children to help her at home. Knowing that helping her would make her happy, some children choose to obey her request. However, some children refuse to obey, making their mothers sad and angry with them.

From this example, you can see that Allāh ﷻ has given the people the freedom to choose good or bad. He loves those who do good and is angered by those who do wrong.

The Qur'ān says:

وَنَفْسٍ وَمَا سَوَّىٰهَا ﴿٧﴾ فَأَلْهَمَهَا فُجُورَهَا وَتَقْوَىٰهَا ﴿٨﴾ قَدْ
أَفْلَحَ مَن زَكَّىٰهَا ﴿٩﴾ وَقَدْ خَابَ مَن دَسَّىٰهَا ﴿١٠﴾

And (by) the soul and Him Who perfected it, and inspired it (with conscious of) what is wrong for it and (what is) right for it. Indeed, he succeeds, who purifies it (his soul) and he is indeed a failure who corrupts it.
(*Ash-Shams* 91: 7-10)

Allāh ﷻ has given humans the gift of His guidance. He has promised to help those who ask Him and sincerely try to obey Him. Allāh ﷻ has also given humans the freedom to turn away from His guidance. Some people choose not to be guided by Allāh ﷻ and they try to guide themselves. Such people go astray and will never be happy in this world or in the next.

It is important to understand that our conscience, the voice of our soul, is the most valuable possession we have. A child is born with a pure soul. As long as he believes in Allāh ﷻ and tries to do good, his soul will stay pure and bright, like a mirror. But if he chooses to ignore Allāh's guidance and behaves in a manner that his conscience knows is wrong, his soul will resemble a mirror that has been covered with dirt. He will have lost sight of Allāh's guiding light and will be left in eternal darkness. It is for this reason that Allāh ﷻ commands us to pray to Him everyday. Consider the words of *Sūrah al-Fātiḥah* (1: 6-7):

اهْدِنَا الصِّرَاطَ الْمُسْتَقِيمَ صِرَاطَ الَّذِينَ أَنْعَمْتَ
عَلَيْهِمْ غَيْرِ الْمَغْضُوبِ عَلَيْهِمْ وَلَا الضَّالِّينَ ﴿٧﴾

Guide us on the right path: the path of those to whom You have given Your blessings.Not the path of those who earn Your anger, nor of those who go astray.
(*Sūrah al-Fātiḥah* 1: 6-7)

✔ EXERCISES

1. Why did Allāh ﷻ give humans intelligence and understanding?
2. Can a person choose to do good or bad?
3. Can a man guide himself without Allāh's guidance?
4. What happens in this world to the soul of someone who does not care about Allāh ﷻ and does bad things?

INTRODUCTORY NOTES ON FIQH FOR TEACHERS

In treating the subject of *Fiqh* at the junior level, the author was faced with a dilemma. If the subject is treated properly, it is quite complex, and young learners may have some difficulty in following the text. However, if the subject is simplified too much, it could lead to errors and omissions in the performance of their religious duties. This latter danger seems to be more serious than the former, especially since the primary/junior levels marks the end of formal Islamic education for some students.

Therefore, the text focuses on information necessary to perform necessary daily rituals. It is left to the teacher to present the information in a way commensurate with the comprehension level of the young students. We suggest the teacher give practical demonstrations and test the students practical applications whenever possible.

The information given was originally written according to the Māliki school of *Fiqh*. IQRA' Foundation has expanded the text to include other schools of *Fiqh*. This broadened perspective will greatly facilitate the teaching of Islāmic *Fiqh* within the realm of the classroom, which often represents a microcosm of all the schools of Fiqh.

The modern world has evolved into a "global village." Both through instruction and experiences with one another, we learn about different religions, cultures, and civilizations. In contrast, our knowledge of the various schools of *Fiqh* is lamentably limited at best. In the United States and the rest of the Western world, the Muslim community has an opportunity to expand its educational horizons while learning to respect differences and appreciate the rich diversity of Islāmic Civilization.

Islāmic Studies teachers have a special responsibility to impart Islāmic knowledge and mold the character of their students in order to fully develop their human and Islāmic potential. The teacher is a role model for the students, so exercising tolerance and appreciation for diversity must not only be reflected in teaching material but also in the personal attitude of the instructor. Only then, will the teachings have real impact on students.

FIQH

LESSON 1

INTRODUCTION TO FIQH & FIVE PILLARS OF ISLĀM

What is Fiqh?

Fiqh is Islāmic jurisprudence. It describes the details of our Islāmic duties and how to perform them.

The Five Pillars of Islām

Islām is based on Five Pillars. The Five Pillars of Islām are:

1. *Kalimah ash-Shahādah*: declaration of faith
2. *Ṣalāh*: prayer
3. *Ṣawm:* fasting
4. *Zakāh*: welfare fees; obligatory charity
5. *Ḥajj*: pilgrimage

The Purpose of the Five Pillars

Pillars are solid structures that hold up the roof of a building. Each pillar needs to be equally strong to do the job effectively. If some pillars are weak, the whole building becomes unstable and may fall apart.

Similarly, practicing the Five Pillars of Islām upholds the *'Īmān* (Faith) of the believer and gives structure to his life. The Five Pillars of Islām describe the most essential forms of worship to Allāh ﷻ. If a person does not take care to uphold the Five Pillars, his *'Īmān* will weaken, and he will become distanced from Allāh ﷻ. In such a vulnerable state, he may easily be led astray by the Shaiṭān and lose all happiness in this world and in the Hereafter.

The Importance of the Five Pillars

If a Muslim observes the Five Pillars of Islām sincerely, Allāh ﷻ will reward him by guiding him on the right path and strengthening his *'Imān*. Thus, learning the correct way of performing these important tasks is essential to leading a successful Islāmic life.

The first of the Five Pillars is *Kalimah ash-Shahādah* ("Declaration of Faith"), which is the affirmation of one's faith in Allāh ﷻ and Rasūlullāh ﷺ as His last prophet. *Tawḥīd* has been discussed in the first section of this book. This section of the book (*Fiqh*) will elaborate on the remaining four pillars of Islām and some other important points of *Fiqh* and *Sharī'ah* (Islāmic Law).

✔ EXERCISES

1. What is *Fiqh*?
2. What are the Five Pillars of Islām?
3. What is the purpose of practicing the Five Pillars of Islām?
4. What is a pillar, and what does it do?
5. What are the results of failing to practice the Five Pillars of Islām?

LESSON 2

PURIFICATION AND ITS MEANS

What Is Meant By Purification?

Before offering prayer, a Muslim must purify himself. He must wash his body and cleanse his heart, mind, and soul in preparation for prayer.

There are three types of purification:

(a) *Wuḍū'* (Ablution)
(b) *Ghusl* (Ritual Bath)
(c) *Tayammum* (Dry Ablution)

Each type will be described in detail in the following lessons.

Determining the Purity of Water

Wuḍū' (Ablution) and *Ghusl* (Ritual Bath) should be performed with pure water. To be considered pure, water should be free of color, taste, or smell. However, if any of these things come from dirt, rocks, salt, or other naturally occurring sources, the water may be used. Furthermore, according to Ḥanafī *Fiqh*, if any pure substance is mixed with water, the water can still be used for *Wuḍū'* or *Ghusl,* as long as two of the three qualities (i.e. color, taste, or smell) have not been changed.

Sources of Pure Water

The following sources of water are considered acceptable for *Wuḍū'* and *Ghusl*: springs, wells, rivers, rain water, melted ice or snow, and sea water.

Cleanliness of Body, Clothes and Place of Worship

As Muslims, we are required to observe basic hygiene. Each time we go to the bathroom, we must clean ourselves with water, if it is available. If water is unavailable, we may use toilet paper. If we are outdoors, or away from a modern toilet, we may use leaves or stones to clean ourselves. When preparing for prayer, in addition to performing *Wuḍū'* or *Ghusl,* we must also ensure that our clothes are clean. This shows our respect for the *Masjid* and for our fellow Muslims.

Before beginning the prayer, we must make sure that the place of worship is clean. We cannot pray in a place that contains *najāsah* (grave impurity).

✔ EXERCISES

1. What is the meaning of purification for prayer?
2. Name the three types of purification.
3. List the requirements for water to be suitable for purification.
4. Name five sources of pure water.
5. How can a Muslim ensure that his body and clothes are always clean for prayer?
6. Is it allowed to offer prayers (*Ṣalāh*) in the washroom? Why or why not?

LESSON 3

THE BENEFITS OF WUḌŪ'

Wuḍū' As Prescribed in the Qur'ān

Allāh ﷿ has prescribed *Wuḍū'* in the following passage of the Qur'ān:

يَٰٓأَيُّهَا ٱلَّذِينَ ءَامَنُوٓا۟ إِذَا قُمْتُمْ إِلَى ٱلصَّلَوٰةِ فَٱغْسِلُوا۟
وُجُوهَكُمْ وَأَيْدِيَكُمْ إِلَى ٱلْمَرَافِقِ وَٱمْسَحُوا۟ بِرُءُوسِكُمْ
وَأَرْجُلَكُمْ إِلَى ٱلْكَعْبَيْنِ ۚ

O you who have attained faith! When you are about to pray, wash your face, and your hands (and arms) up to the elbows; rub your heads (with water); and (wash) your feet to ankles.
(*Al-Mā'idah* 5:6)

Preparation of the Body

The *Wuḍū'* prepares our bodies for prayer. We are about to stand before Allāh ﷿, our Creator, Lord and King, and we should try to present ourselves in the best way possible. By washing ourselves, ensuring that our clothes are clean and tidy, and making ourselves calm and attentive, we humbly show that we are ready to be in Allāh's presence.

Preparation of the Mind

The *Wuḍū'* prepares a Muslim mentally and spiritually for prayer. When we wash the dirt from our bodies, we may imagine washing away the sins from our bodies and souls. We must also have the intention not to repeat our sins.

So, when we wash our hands, we should repent any wrong deeds that we may have done with our hands. When we wash our mouths, we should repent any wrong things we may have said, and so on.

If we prepare ourselves for prayer in this way, we become more attentive to the purpose of the prayer and it brings us closer to Allāh ﷻ.

`Uthmān ibn `Affān ؓ reported that the Prophet ﷺ said:

> *He who makes Wuḍū' and makes it in the best way,*
> *his sins leave his body, even from beneath his nails.*
> (Transmitted by Muslim)

✔ EXERCISES

1. Describe how you would prepare yourself to stand before your Creator.
2. How can a Muslim make *Wuḍū'* in the best way, so that he washes off his sins as well as his dirt?

LESSON 4

THE SIGNIFICANCE OF EACH ACT OF WUḌŪ'

We have learned that *Wuḍū* is an important way a Muslim purifies himself in preparation for worship. Each act of *Wuḍū* carries its own significance. Some acts are more essential than others. Let us examine these acts in more detail.

Farāiḍ-al-Wuḍū': Seven Compulsory Acts of Ablution

Some of the acts of *Wuḍū'* are *Farḍ* (obligatory). If one of these required acts is omitted, one must go back to complete it, and then repeat the remaining acts of *Wuḍū'* up to the end. In the Ḥanafī *madhhab,* one must go back and complete only the part that was omitted; and the remaining parts of the *Wuḍū'* need not be repeated. If the person has already prayed by the time he remembers that he has omitted a *Farḍ* act, he should repeat the whole *Wuḍū'* and the prayer. The four *Farḍ* acts of *Wuḍū'* are mentioned in the Qur'ān. We will look at these in detail over the next few lessons.

Sunan-al-Wuḍū': The Necessary Acts of Ablution by the Tradition of Rasūlullāh ﷺ

Certain acts of *Wuḍū'* are very important, because they were practiced by Rasūlullāh ﷺ. These *Sunnah* acts of *Wuḍū'* are called *Sunan al-Wuḍū'ī.* If one of these acts is missed, it should be completed; although it is not necessary to repeat the *Wuḍū'*. According to the Ḥanafī *madhhab,* any *Sunnah* act which is missed does not nullify the *Ṣalāh.*

If one does not remember that he missed a *Sunan al-Wuḍū'ī* until after completing the prayer, his prayer is still valid. However, he should perform a fresh, complete *Wuḍū'* before offering the next obligatory prayer.

Mustaḥabbāt-al-Wuḍū': Recommended Acts of *Wuḍū'*

There are about five to ten other small acts which are recommended, because they make the *Wuḍū'* more perfect. However, if they are not included, the *Wuḍū'* is still valid.

A summary of the various acts of *Wuḍū* according to their respective significance and the order that they should be performed can be found on the next page.

ACTS OF ABLUTION	FARḌ	SUNNAH	MUSTAḤAB
Say: *Bismillāh-ar-Rahmān-ar-Rahīm*			✔
Intention	✔		
Washing the hands		✔	
Rinsing the mouth		✔	
Sniffing water & blowing it out		✔	
Washing the face	✔		
Washing the arms	✔		
Wiping the head, from front to back		✔	
Wiping the head, neck to hairline		✔	
Wetting the hands to rub the ears.		✔	
Rubbing the ears		✔	
Washing the feet	✔		
Declaration of Faith			✔
Rubbing thoroughly when washing	✔		
Not interrupting *Wuḍū'*	✔		
Doing the acts of ablution in order		✔	
Brushing the teeth before ablution			✔
Repetition three times of each act			✔
Choosing a clean place for ablution			✔
Not wasting water in ablution			✔

✔ EXERCISES

1. What are the seven *Farā'iḍ al-Wuḍū'*?
2. What are the eight *Sunan al-Wuḍū'*?
3. Name five of the *Mustaḥabbāt al-Wuḍū'*.
4. If a person forgets a *Farḍ* act of *Wuḍū'* and remembers it just *after* completing it, what should he do?
5. If a person forgets a *Farḍ* act of *Wuḍū'* and remembers it *after* offering the prayer, what should he do?
6. If a person forgets a *Sunan al-Wuḍū'* and remembers it *after* offering the prayer, what should he do?
7. Why should the *Mustaḥabbāt al-Wuḍū'* be done?

LESSON 5

HOW TO PERFORM WUḌŪ' (Ablution)

Step 1 Start with the name of Allāh ﷻ by reciting: *Bismillāhi (A)r-Raḥmāni (A)r-Raḥīm(i)*, which means: "In the name of Allāh, the Beneficent, the Merciful." (*Sunnah*)

Step 2 Make the intention of purifying yourself for worship. This can be done silently and in your own language. In all the *madhāhib*, except the Ḥanafī, this step is required for the *Wuḍū'* to be complete. (*Farḍ)*

Step 3 Wash the right hand, then the left hand. You should wash up to the wrist and between the fingers. Doing this three times is recommended. (*Farḍ*)

Step 4 Rinse the mouth. Three times is recommended.(*Mustaḥab*)

Step 5 Sniff water into the nose, and blow it out gently. Three times is recommended. (*Mustaḥab*)

Step 6 Wash the face, from hairline to chin, and from ear to ear. According to all the Sunni *madhāhib,* it is best to wash from the top of the face downwards, but it may be done in any manner. Doing this three times is recommended. (*Farḍ*)

Step 7 Wash the right arm up to the elbow three times. Repeat with the left arm. According to the Ḥanafī, Mālikī, Shāfi`ī and Hanbalī *madhāhib,* one should wash from the hands up to the elbows. Three times is recommended. (*Farḍ*)

Step 8 Make *masaḥ* of the head. According to the Mālikī and Hanbalī *madhhāhib,* wet your hands and rub the head once from the front hairline to the back of the neck and back again to the front. According to the Ḥanafī *madhhab,* only one-fourth of the head need be wiped with the wet hands. According to the Shāfi 'i *madhhab,* it is required that the entire head, not missing even a single hair, be wiped with wet hands. In all of the *madhāhib,* one may make *masaḥ* over a *ṭaqīyyah* (cap) or turban.(*Sunnah*)

Step 9 (*Sunnah*) Make *masaḥ* of the neck. According to the Ḥanafī *madhhab,* wet the hands and rub the ears, front and back, once. Then the back of the neck should be wiped. This should all be considered one step. The wiping of the ears is mandatory in the Hanbalī *madhhab*, but considered recommended in the others.

Step 10 In the four Sunnī *madhāhib,* we wash the feet from the toes to the heels and ankles, starting with the right foot. Remember to rub between the toes. Doing this three times is recommended.

Step 11 To complete the *Wuḍū',* recite the Declaration of Faith (*Kalimah ash-Shahādah*):

أَشْهَدُ أَلاَّ اِلَهِ الاَّ اللَّهُ وَحْدَهُ لا شَرِيكَ لَهُ
وَ أَشْهَدُ اَنَّ مُحَمَّدًا عَبْدُهُ وَرَسُوْلُهُ

Ashhadu 'an lā ilāha illa allāhu Waḥdahu lā sharīka la-h(u) wa ashhadu 'anna Muḥammadan `abdu-hu wa Rasūluh(u).

I bear witness that there is no god but Allāh, One and without partner, and I bear witness that Muhammad is His servant and messenger.

Summary of Wuḍū'

According to the S̲h̲āfi'ī and Hanbalī, it is *Farḍ* to make *Wuḍū'* in the prescribed order. According to the Ḥanafī and Mālikī *madh̲āhib*, it is *mustaḥab* to do so.

1. Start with ***Bismillāhi (A)r-Raḥmāni (A)r-Raḥīm(I)***
2. Make **intention**.
3. Wash **hands**.
4. Rinse **mouth**.
5. Sniff water in **nose**.
6. Wash **face**.
7. Wash **arms**.
8. Make *masaḥ* of **head**.
9. Make *masaḥ* of **ears**.
10. Wash **feet**.
11. Recite ***As̲h̲-S̲h̲ahādah***.

✔ EXERCISES

1. What is said in Arabic when you start your *Wuḍū'*?
2. Is the intention made out loud or silently?
3. What would you say in your intention to perform *Wuḍū'*?
4. Describe and demonstrate the acts of *Wuḍū'*.
5. What should you say in Arabic when you have completed the *Wuḍū'*, and what is its meaning?
6. Summarize the order of *Wuḍū'*, according to the *madh̲hab* you follow.

THE PROCEDURE FOR WUḌŪ'

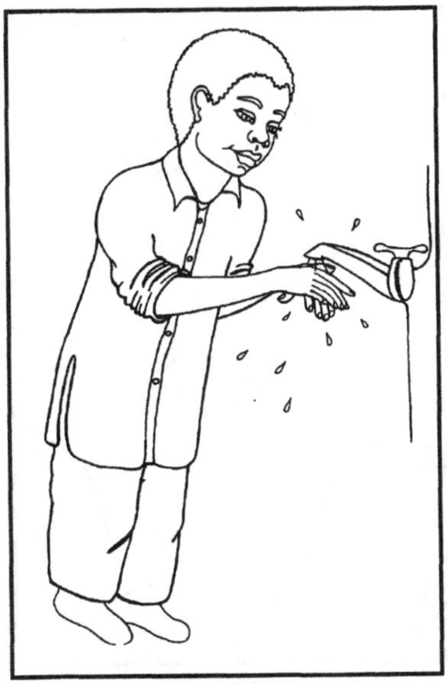

STEP 1,2,&3
Starting with *Bismillāh*, make the intention, wash the hands to the wrists.
(Three times is preferred)

STEP 4
Rinse the mouth. (Three times preferred)

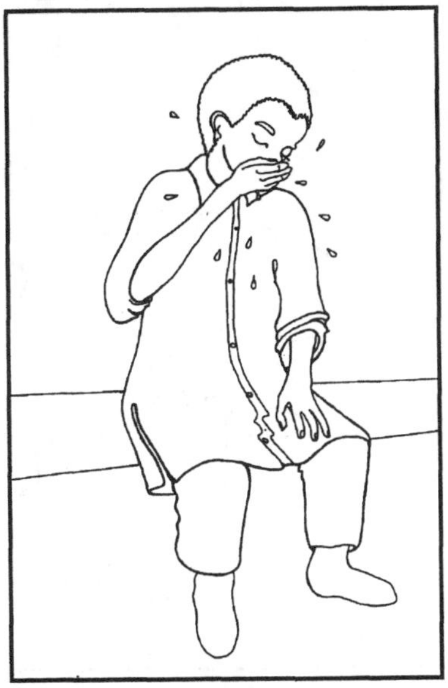

STEP 5
Sniff water in nose. (Three times preferred)

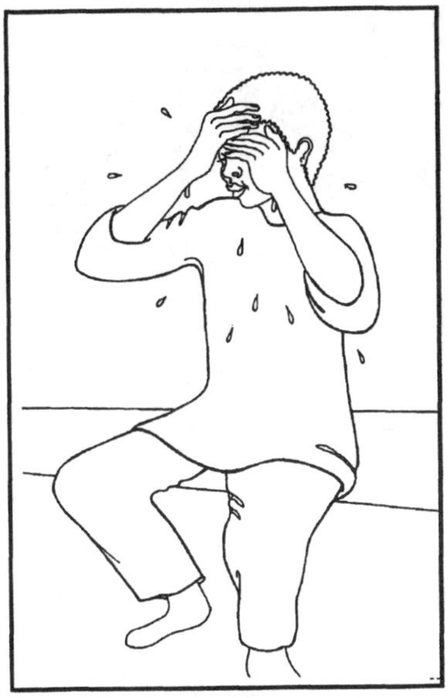

STEP 6
Wash face. (Three times preferred)

STEP 7
Wash arms to elbow. (Three times preferred)

STEP 8
Make *Masah* of the head.

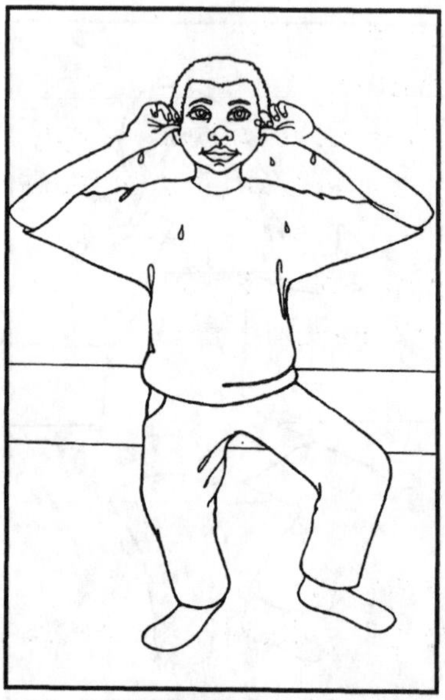

STEP 9
Make *Masah* of the ears.

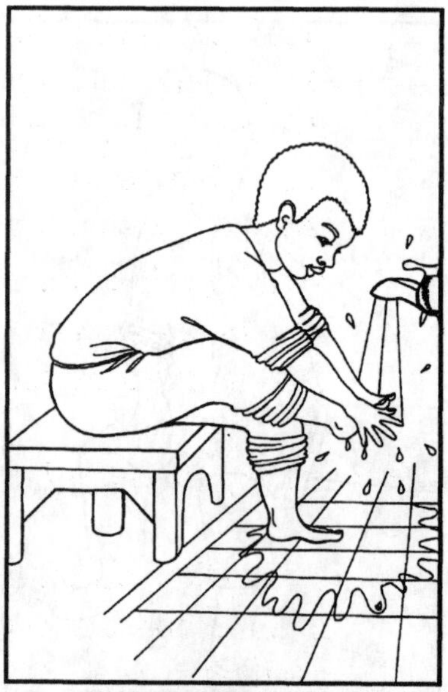

STEP 10 & 11
Wash both feet to ankles.
End with *Ash-Shahādah*.

LESSON 6

CONDITIONS THAT NULLIFY WUḌŪ'

According to the **Mālikī *madhhab*,** the following conditions nullify the *Wuḍū'*:

1. Defecation, urination, or passing gas.
2. Deep sleep, whether for a short or long while.
3. Loss of one's senses due to fainting, madness or drinking alcohol.
4. Emission of semen.
5. Touching the uncovered private parts with the palm of the hand or fingers.
6. Having doubts about whether one's *Wuḍū'* is valid.

According to the Ḥanafī ***madhhab,*** these conditions would nullify the *Wuḍū'*:

1. Passing of gas or fluid from any part of the body
2. Deep sleep in a reclining position. Sleeping in the sitting, standing or kneeling position does not break the *Wuḍū'*.
3. Loss of senses due to fainting, madness or drunkenness
4. Vomiting a mouthful
5. Spitting saliva that is made up of mostly blood
6. Touching ones private parts with the bare hand
7. Laughing during the prayer

According to the Shāfi'ī ***madhhab:***

1. Defecation, urination or passing of gas
2. Losing consciousness or sleeping deeply in the reclining position
3. Touching the private parts with the bare hand.

4. Touching the skin of someone of the opposite sex who is not related to you.

According to the **Hanbalī *madhhab***:

1. Going to the bathroom or passing gas
2. Deep sleep in any position
3. Emission of semen
4. Vomiting a mouthful
5. Large amounts of blood or pus discharged from the body
6. Eating the meat of an animal not slaughtered in the name of Allāh ﷻ

Under any of these conditions, it becomes necessary to repeat *Wuḍū'* before the next prayer.

Conditions for Which Wuḍū' is Necessary

A Muslim is required to have *Wuḍū'* in the following circumstances:

1. To make *Ṣalāh* of any kind
2. To make *Ṭawāf* around the Ka`bah
3. To make *Sajdah* when reading certain *Āyāt* of the Qur'ān
4. To touch the Arabic text of the Qur'ān

✔ EXERCISES

1. List from memory all the conditions which nullify *Wuḍū'*.
2. When is a Muslim required to make *Wuḍū'*?
3. What are the three conditions common to all Madhāhib which nullify the *Wuḍū'*?

LESSON 7

THE GHUSL

The *Ghusl* is a ritual bath performed to purify one's body for prayer and other acts of worship.

What Necessitates the Ghusl?

Just as *Wuḍū'* is necessary to remove a minor impurity, *Ghusl* is necessary to remove a greater impurity. The following occasions make *Ghusl* necessary:

1. When a woman's monthly period ends.
2. When a woman's blood of childbirth ends.
3. After emission of semen, whether the male is awake or asleep.
4. After sexual intercourse with one's spouse.
5. According to the Hanbalī school of thought, any non-Muslim who becomes a Muslim *must* perform *Ghusl*. The Shāfi'ī *madhhab* require that a new Muslim perform *Ghusl* only if one of the above conditions occurred before the *Shahādah* is recited.

How to Perform Ghusl

Step 1 Start with: *Bismillāhi (A)r-Raḥmāni (A)r-Raḥīm(I)*, which means: "In the name of Allāh, the Beneficent, the Merciful." According to the Ḥanafī *madhhab,* this is not to be recited if the *Ghusl* is *Farḍ.*

Step 2 Make intention silently for performing *Ghusl* to purify your body for worship. The Ḥanafīs do not consider this step mandatory.

Step 3 Wash the *najāsah* from the private parts.

Step 4 Perform *Wuḍū'* as taught in Lesson 4, but wash each part only once.

Step 5 Wash the entire body from head to toe. It is best (*mustaḥab*) to wash from the top to the bottom, and the right to the left. All Ḥanafīs are required to rinse the mouth and the nose during the *Ghusl.*

After Step 4 above (*i.e. Wuḍū'*), avoid touching the private parts with the inside of the hand. If you do so, it will become necessary to perform *Wuḍū'* again before *Ṣalāh*. This is not necessary in the Ḥanafī *madhhab.*

✔ EXERCISES

1. What is the *Ghusl*?
2. What necessitates the *Ghusl*?
3. What should an adult who becomes a Muslim do before he offers his first prayer?
4. What are the steps of the *Ghusl*, in their correct order?
5. What are the *Farḍ* acts of the *Ghusl*?

LESSON 8

TAYAMMUM

Tayammum is a dry *Wuḍū'*, using dust instead of water.

When is Tayammum Performed?

It may be performed in place of *Wuḍū'* or the *Ghusl* in the following circumstances:

1. When there is no water.
2. When there is scarcity of water.
3. When it is dangerous to go to the place of water.
4. When the water is at a very distant place.
5. During illness, when washing with water will increase the illness or delay recover.

Obviously, *Tayammum* is to be performed only in an emergency. According to most of the *madhāhib,* it remains valid only for one prayer and must be repeated for each subsequent prayer. In the Ḥanafī *madhhab, Tayammum* remains valid for as long as any of the conditions above are in effect; however, if any of the circumstances that would normally break *Wuḍū'* occurs, *Tayammum* becomes void.

If someone has prayed with *Tayammum,* and then water becomes available before the end of the time of that prayer, he should make *Wuḍū'* or bathe with water and repeat the prayer. If the prayer time passes without the water being available, the prayer with *Tayammum* is valid. However, according to the Ḥanafī *madhhab*, even if water is found before the end of the prayer time, once the prayer has been completed, it does not have to be repeated.

THE PROCEDURE FOR TAYAMMUM

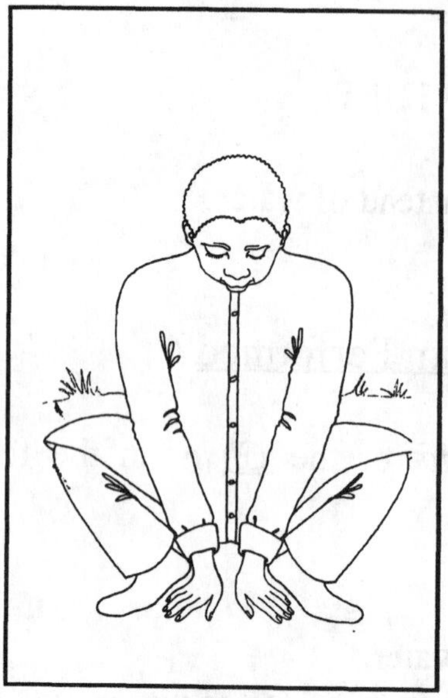

STEP 1-4
Using a clean area of earth and starting with *Bismillāh*, make intention for *Tayammum*. Press hands on grounds surface.

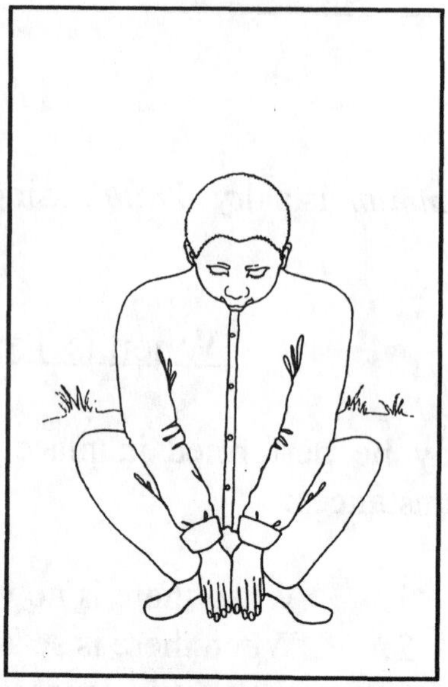

STEP 5
Lift hands as shown, palms downwards, gently hitting their sides together to knock off extra dust.

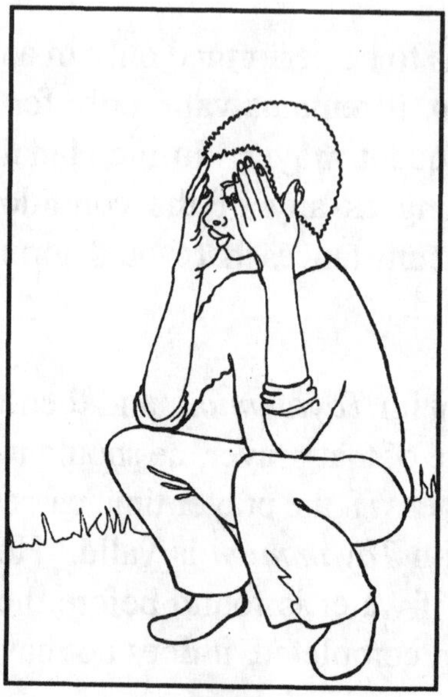

STEP 6
Rub your face with your hands.

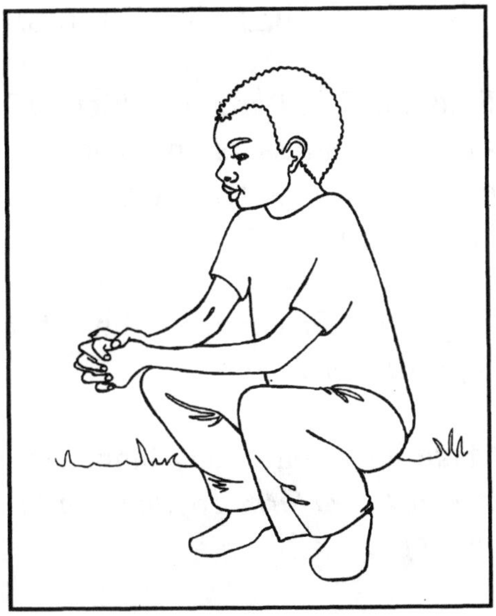

STEP 7

Press your hands to the ground again, shaking off extra dust, as in Step 5. Rub hands together.

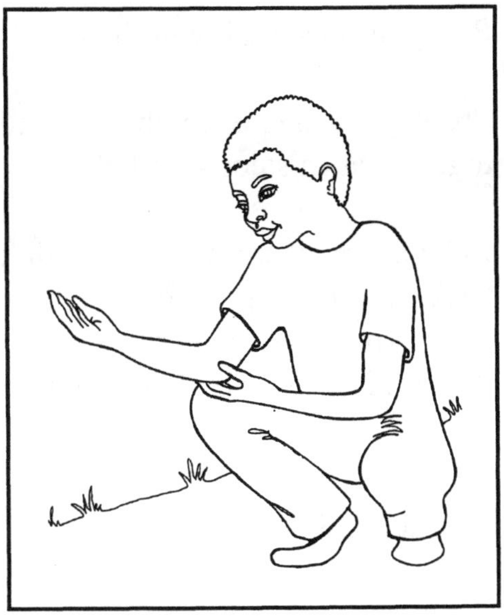

STEP 8

Rub your right arm with your left hand, starting from the back of the finders to the elbow, and back along the inner arm to the hand, rubbing between the fingers. Repeat with the other arm.

How to Perform Tayammum

Step 1 Find a piece of ground which is free of *najāsah*: rock, sand, dust, grass, or any other natural surface. Sand or dust may also be fetched from another place to perform *Tayammum.*

Step 2 Begin the *Tayammum* with "*Bismillāhi (A)r-Raḥmāni (A)r-Raḥīm(i)*"

Step 3 Make intention in any language, silently declaring: "*I intend to perform Tayammum to enable me to offer a ritual prayer.*"

Step 4 Press the hands on the ground's surface.

Step 5 Lift your hands as shown, palms downwards, gently hitting their sides together to knock off surplus dust.

Step 6 Rub your face with your hands.

Step 7 Press your hands to the ground and hit their sides together as in steps 4 and 5.

Step 8 Rub your right arm with your left hand, starting from the back of your fingers to the elbow, and back along the inner arm to the hand, remembering to rub between the fingers. Repeat with your other arm.

Summary of Tayammum

1. ***Bismillāhi (A)r-Raḥmāni (A)r-Raḥīm(i)***
2. **Intention**
3. Press **hands on dust** and knock hands together

4. Rub **face**
5. Press **hands on dust** and knock hands together
6. Rub **right arm, then left**

Conditions That Nullify Tayammum

The same conditions that nullify *Wuḍū'* also render *Tayammum* void (see Lesson 5).

✔ EXERCISES

1. Describe five circumstances in which *Tayammum* instead of *Wuḍū'* or *Ghusl*
2. For how many prayers is the *Tayammum* valid?
3. If a person prays *'Ishā'* at 8:30 p.m. with *Tayammum* because there is no water, and water then becomes available at 9:30 p.m., what should he do?
4. List the acts of *Tayammum* in their correct order.
5. What nullifies *Tayammum*?

LESSON 9

THE ṢALĀH

What is the Value of Ṣalāh to Muslims?

Ṣalāh, or prayer, is the second Pillar of Islām. *Ṣalāh* offers us the opportunity to communicate with God directly at any time and place. It is a time for reflection and evaluation of our past actions and preparation for future actions. As we shall see, *Ṣalāh* is important for both individual growth and community solidarity.

Worship is the Purpose of Creation

Allāh ﷻ says in the Qur'ān:

وَمَا خَلَقْتُ ٱلْجِنَّ وَٱلْإِنسَ إِلَّا لِيَعْبُدُونِ ﴿٥٦﴾

I have only created jinn and men that they may worship Me.
(*Al-Zāriyāt* 51:56)

It is human nature to seek a higher power for worship. Deep down, every human being feels the existence of God. This is evident by the existence of so many religions in the world today. However, as promised in the Qur'ān, God's true, unchanged word, only Islām shows us the meaning of true worship. True worship is complete submission of heart, soul, mind, and body to the Will of Allāh ﷻ. *Ṣalāh* provides a means of submission, allowing human beings to carry out the purpose for which they were created.

The Ṣalāh is a Reminder of Allāh ﷻ:

We often become very busy in our daily routines: we go to school, we do our chores, we play with our friends, we spend time with our families, etc. With all this activity, sometimes it can be hard to remember Allāh ﷾. When our minds are busy elsewhere, the Shaiṭān finds weakness and tries to distract us from remembering Allāh ﷾.

This is why *Ṣalāh* is so important. When we pray, we focus on remembering Allāh ﷾. We praise Him for His mercy and kindness, and we remember that He is our Master and King on the Day of Judgement. We ask Him to guide us on the right path and protect us from the temptations of the Shaiṭān.

The Qur'ān says:

إِنَّ ٱلصَّلَوٰةَ تَنْهَىٰ عَنِ ٱلْفَحْشَآءِ وَٱلْمُنكَرِ

Indeed, the prayer prevents one from shameful and unjust acts.
(*Al-`Ankabūt* 29:45)

Praying five times every day keeps our *'Īmān* strong and makes us more conscious of Allāh ﷾. The more aware we are of His presence, watching our every action, the more we avoid breaking His laws and become better people. Rasūlullāh ﷺ advised:

Worship your Lord as if you see Him, and if you cannot do that, then know that He sees you.
(Transmitted by Bukhārī)

The Ṣalāh Expresses Humility Before Allāh ﷾

In Islām, prayer includes both words and movements which are intended to express our humility before Allāh ﷾. Thus, regardless of a person's social position or wealth, whether he is a king or a pauper, he must bow and prostrate with his nose and forehead to the ground. Men and women are equal in the eyes of Allāh ﷾, and the prayer helps to remove all feelings of pride and superiority among human beings.

The Ṣalāh is a Formal Communication with Allāh ﷻ

A person engaged in prayer is able to express his needs directly to Allāh ﷻ. Allāh ﷻ says in the Qur'ān:

وَقَالَ رَبُّكُمُ ٱدْعُونِيٓ أَسْتَجِبْ لَكُمْ ۚ

Call on Me, and I shall answer your call.
(*Ghāfir* 40:60)

Ṣalāh empowers a Muslim by bringing him closer to Allāh ﷻ. When offering the *Ṣalāh*, he can feel Allāh's power firsthand. His reward will be hope and tranquillity, and the knowledge that Allāh ﷻ will help him face and overcome the difficulties that are troubling him.

The Ṣalāh Strengthens the Islāmic Community

It is strongly recommended that Muslims offer the *Ṣalāh* in *Jamā'ah* (congregation), whether at home with the family, in the *Masjid*, or anywhere else where Muslims find themselves together at the time of prayer.

Praying together helps foster the feeling of brotherhood among Muslims. Muslims pray for Allāh's guidance and blessings. They share the common bond of service to Allāh ﷻ. So naturally, they develop love and understanding for each other. Kindness to each other and regard for each other's needs becomes as much a part of worship as *Ṣalāh*. As each individual Muslim becomes a better person, the Muslim community improves spiritually, and consequently, the human society as a whole benefits.

The Ṣalāh Teaches Punctuality, Cooperation and Discipline

When the time for *Ṣalāh* approaches, we should not delay in offering the prayer. All other activities must be stopped, and the *Ṣalāh* should become our first priority. Any delay will give the Shaiṭān the opportunity to mislead us away from *Ṣalāh*.

Praying *Ṣalāh* in *Jamā'ah* is a lesson in cooperation and orderliness. The one who is most learned leads as *Imām*. The followers line up in straight lines, shoulder to shoulder, like soldiers. When the *Imām* gives the call, the group follows him as one body. If the *Imām* makes a mistake during the prayer, one of the followers should correct him politely in the prescribed manner. Thus, even though the *Imām* is the leader, every follower carries a responsibility for his own *Ṣalāh* and the *Ṣalāh* of his fellow followers.

The benefits and blessings of the *Ṣalāh* in Islām are too numerous to mention here. Those given above are just a few examples.

✔ EXERCISES

1. Explain some reasons why a Muslim must offer the *Ṣalāh*.
2. How does the *Ṣalāh* help a Muslim in his or her daily life?
3. How does the *Ṣalāh* help strengthen the Muslim community?
4. What useful lessons in behavior do we learn from: (a) prayer at regular intervals throughout the day; (b) prayer in *Jamā`ah*?

LESSON 10

THE FIVE COMPULSORY PRAYERS

The Five Daily Prayers Should Never Be Neglected

The five daily *Ṣalawāt* (prayers) should never be neglected. If a person is too ill to stand, he may pray sitting. If he is too ill to sit, he may pray lying down. Prayer is the most important link between the believer and Allāh ﷻ. If a person is negligent of his *Ṣalāh,* he is breaking communication with Allāh ﷻ.

Exemption from Prayers

The only adult Muslims who are excused from the *Farḍ* prayers are: (a) woman during her monthly period or during the blood of childbirth; (b) a mentally incapacitated person; (c) an unconscious person. Those who fall into these categories do not need to make up the missed prayers when they have purified themselves or are recovered.

The Age at Which Children Should Pray

Often, young children imitate their parents when they pray. This should be encouraged. The best way for children to learn the steps of *Ṣalāh* is by following the example of their parents, elder brothers and sisters, and other relatives.

Children should be encouraged to pray from the age of seven. From the age of ten, they may be punished if they refuse to pray. It is a sin for any Muslim who has reached the age of puberty to deliberately omit a *Farḍ* prayer.

The Five Daily Ṣalawāt

The five daily *Ṣalawāt* in order are:

1. *Fajr* or *Ṣubḥ* (dawn)
2. *Ẓuhr* (afternoon)
3. *'Aṣr* (mid-afternoon)
4. *Maghrib* (after sunset)
5. *'Ishā'* (twilight)

The Times of the Five Daily Ṣalawāt

Each prayer has an appointed time. A Muslim should always make sure to pray each prayer at its appointed time. The appointed time and the extension time of each prayer is as follows:

PRAYER	TIMINGS
Fajr (Dawn)	From dawn until the sky turns bright yellow
Zuhr (Afternoon)	From after mid-day until mid-afternoon, i.e., when the length of an object's shadow is double it's actual size.
'Asr (Mid-afternoon)	From the time that an object's shadow becomes double its size until just before sunset.
Maghrib (Sunset)	Immediately after sunset until just before twilight (the sky turns completely dark)
'Ishā' (Night)	From twilight to dawn, although the preferred time is before one-third of the night has passed

✔ EXERCISES

1. How should a sick person pray?
2. Name three conditions under which a Muslim is excused from the

Ṣalāh.

3. If a woman's monthly period has ended, and she has performed the *Ghusl* (Ritual Bath), does she have to make up for the prayers she missed during her period?
4. From what age should a Muslim child be admonished if he or she refuses to pray?
5. What are the names of the five daily *Ṣalawāt* in Arabic, and their English translation?
6. Describe the appointed time and the extension time for each of the five daily *Ṣalawāt*.

LESSON 11

THE 'ADHĀN AND THE QIBLAH

The 'Adhān and the Mu'adhdhin

The *'Adhān* should be called at the time of prayer in the mosque, in the home or anywhere else that Muslims gather for the *Ṣalāh*. The person who calls the *'Adhān* is called a *Mu'adhdhin.*

The *'Adhān* reminds Muslims that it is time for the *Ṣalāh*. When a Muslim hears the *'Adhān,* he should leave whatever he is doing and prepare for the *Ṣalāh.*

It is desirable that the *Mu'adhdhin* have *Wuḍū.* He should go to the top of the minaret (if the mosque has one) or stand from a high place. He should stand facing the *Qiblah* (the direction of the Ka'bah) and call the *'Adhān* in a loud voice. Many mosques have loud speaker systems used for the *'Adhān.*

The Recitation of the 'Adhān and Its Meaning

Allāhu Akbar, Allāhu Akbar	*Allāh is the Greatest!* *Allāh is the Greatest!*
Ashhadu 'an lā ilāha illa (A)llāh ***Ashhadu 'an lā ilāha illa (A)llāh***	*I testify there is no god but Allāh.* *I testify there is no god but Allāh.*
Ashhadu'anna Muḥammada(n)r- Rasūlullāh ***Ashhadu'anna Muḥammada(n)r- Rasūlullāh***	*I testify that Muḥammad is the Messenger of Allāh.* *I testify that Muḥammad is the Messenger of Allāh.*
Ḥayya 'ala (a)ṣ-Ṣalāh	*Hasten to prayer!*

Ḥayya 'ala (a)ṣ-Ṣalāh	*Hasten to prayer!*
Ḥayya 'ala (a)l-falāh	*Hasten to The Success*
Ḥayya 'ala (a)l-falāh	*Hasten to The Success*
Allāhu Akbar, Allāhu Akbar	*Allāh is the Greatest!*
	Allāh is the Greatest!
Lā ilāha illa (A)llāh.	*There is no god but Allāh*

According to the Ḥanafīs, Shāfi'īs, Mālikīs and Hanbalīs, after the second "***Ḥayya 'ala (a)l-falāh***" of the *'Adhān* for the *Fajr Ṣalāh*, the following must be added (repeated twice):

Aṣ-Ṣalātu khairu(n)m min an-nawm	*Prayer is better than sleep.*

Choosing the Appropriate Place for Ṣalāh

The prayer may be offered in a *Masjid*, or any other clean place where Muslims are gathered. We may also make our *Ṣalāh* at home, at a place of business or factory, in the open air or any other convenient, clean location. The most excellent *Ṣalāh* is that which is offered in *Jamā`ah* (congregation).

It is narrated by 'Abdullāh ibn 'Umar ﷺ that Rasūlullāh ﷺ said:

The prayer in congregation is twenty seven times
more superior to the prayer offered by a person alone.
(Transmitted by al-Bukhārī)

Cleanliness and Dress

As emphasized in previous lessons, one should make sure that he or she has *Wuḍū'* in preparation for *Ṣalāh*. The clothes should also be clean and decent. Both boys and girls must cover their *Ṣatr* properly. *Ṣatr* is those parts of the body that must be covered. A man's *Ṣatr* is that area between his navel and his knees. *Satr* for the women includes her whole body except her face, hands, and feet.

The Qiblah

Muslims must face the *Qiblah* when offering the *Ṣalāh*. The *Qiblah* is the direction of Ka`bah in Makkah. The direction of *Qiblah* varies according to the different parts of the world.

In North America, the *Qiblah* is in a southeast direction. In West Africa, the *Qiblah* is in an easterly direction. In Turkey, the *Qiblah* is to the south. In India, Malaysia, and Indonesia, the *Qiblah* is to the west, and in South Africa, the *Qiblah* is to the north.

When Muslims pray in the *Bait al-Ḥaram* in Makkah, they encircle the Ka`bah. All Muslims face the same *Qiblah* in prayer. The Ka`bah is a symbol of Muslim brotherhood and unity even though the *Ummah* (Muslim community) is scattered throughout the world.

The Ka`bah, located in the *Bait al-Ḥaram,* is the most sacred place of worship in Islām. It was a place chosen by Allāh ﷻ, Who directed first prophet, Ādam ؈, and then Prophet Ibrāhīm ؈ and Prophet Ismā`īl ؈, his son, to build a house of worship for His servants.

After a period of time, people began to use the *Masjid* for idol worship. After many centuries, Rasūlullāh ﷺ destroyed the idols and purified the Ka`bah from *Shirk.* Once more, the Ka`bah became *Bait-Allāh,* the House of Allāh ﷻ, to be used for the worship of Allāh ﷻ alone. The Ka`bah was chosen by Allāh ﷻ as the *Qiblah* for all Muslims until the end of time.

✔ EXERCISES

1. What is the meaning of the word *'Adhān?*
2. The *Mu'adhdhin* should face the _____. He should call the prayer in a _____ voice.
3. Recite the *'Adhān* by heart, with its meaning.

4. Which phrase is added to the *'Adhān* of *Fajr*, and what does it mean? Where is it added?
5. Which has greater reward: offering the *Ṣalāh* alone or in *Jamā`ah*? Why?
6. Where should a Muslim offer his *Ṣalāh*?
7. What is the *Qiblah*?
8. What is the Ka`bah?
9. Where is the Ka`bah located?
10. Who first built the Ka`bah?
11. Who later cleaned the idols from the Ka`bah?

LESSON 12

THE 'IQĀMAH AND THE START OF PRAYER

The 'Iqāmah

The *'Iqāmah* is the call to the start of prayer. It is the signal to stand facing the *Qiblah,* ready for the prayer to begin. Although it is not necessary for a person praying alone to recite it, there is merit in doing so. If the *Ṣalāh* is being offered in *Jamā'ah,* any member of the group may call it out loud. However, it is preferable that the *Mu'adhdhin* call the *'Iqāmah.*

The Words of the 'Iqāmah and Their Meaning

The words of the *'Iqāmah,* similar to those of *'Adhān,* are as follows:

Allāhū Akbar, Allāhū Akbar *(2x)*	*Allāh is Most Great! Allāh is Most Great!*
Ashhadu 'an lā ilāha illa (A)llāh *(2x)*	*I testify that there is no god but Allāh.*
Ashhadu 'anna *Muḥammada(n)r-* ***Rasūlullāh*** *(2x)*	*I testify that Muḥammad is the Messenger of Allāh.*
Ḥayya 'ala *(a)ṣ-Ṣ**alāh*** *(2x)*	*Hasten to prayer!*
Ḥayya 'ala (a)l-falāh *(2x)*	*Hasten to success!*
Qad qāmati *(a)ṣ-Ṣ**alāh*** *(2x)*	*Prayer has started!*
Allāhu Akbar! Allāhu Akbar! *(2x)*	*Allāh is the Most Great*

THE POSITION FOR 'IQĀMAH

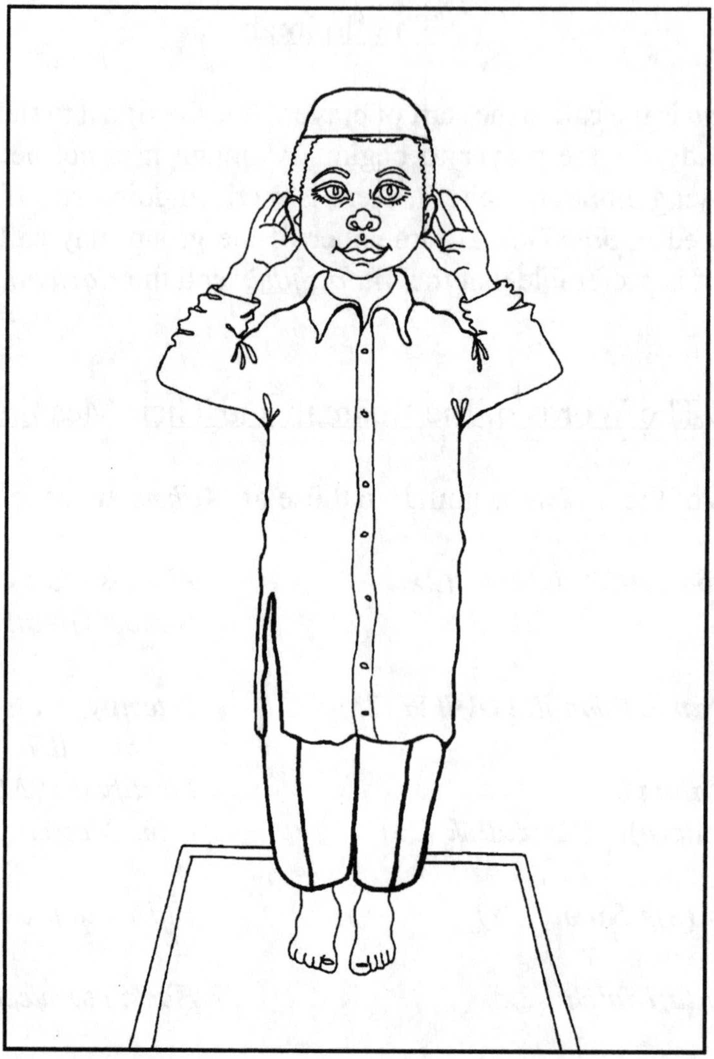

Lā ilāha illa (A)llāh. *(1x)* *There is no god but Allāh*

According to the Shāfi`ī school, it is only required to repeat each line once instead of twice as presented above.

Intention and Takbīrāt al-Iḥrām

The worshiper then makes the intention for the *Ṣalāh* he is going to offer. At the same time, he raises his hands to the level of his ears, or below them, and says:

Allāhū Akbar *Allāh is Most Great.*

The intention should be made silently in any language. For example, one may say: "O Allāh ﷻ, I intend to perform the prescribed *(name of prayer)* prayer with *(number of Raka`āt) Rak`ah*, (type of *Ṣalāh: Farḍ, Sunnah*, or *Nafl*) facing the *Qiblah*," and then begin the first *Rak'ah*.

✔ EXERCISES

1. How should a Muslim dress for prayer?
2. Which parts may remain uncovered by a Muslim woman in prayer?
3. Who should call the *'Iqāmah*?
4. When the *'Iqāmah* is called, what should one do?
5. Recite the *'Iqāmah* with its meaning.
6. What is the opening for prayer? Explain and demonstrate.
7. Describe how you would make the intention for the *Maghrib* prayer (sunset prayer).

LESSON 13

THE FIRST RAK'AH

What is a Rak`ah?

A *Rak'ah* is one unit of the *Ṣalāh.* It consists of a set of recitations and movements that include the following:

1. ***Qiyām***: standing facing the *Qiblah*, individually or in *Jamā`ah.*
2. ***Tilāwah***: recitation of *Al-Fātiḥah* and another *Sūrah* or long *Āyah* (in the first two *Raka'āt* only).
3. ***Rukū`***: bowing.
4. ***Qawmah***: rising from bowing.
5. ***Sajdah***: prostration
6. ***Jalsah***: sitting between the two *Sujūd* (prostrations).

We shall now learn in detail how each part of the *Rak'ah* is done, and what is recited.

The Qiyām: The Standing Position

After making the intention for the prayer and saying ***'Allāhu Akbar'*** (*Takbīrāt al-Iḥrām*), as described in Lesson 12, the worshiper stands with his hands folded just above the navel according to the Ḥanafīs, folded and held higher up by Shāfi'īs and Hanbalīs, and held at the sides by Mālikīs.

The ***thana*** should then be read:

According to Ḥanafī *fiqh*:

سُبْحَانَكَ اللّٰهُمَّ وَبِحَمْدِكَ وَتَبَارَكَ اسْمُكَ

وَتَعَالَى جَدُّكَ وَلَا إِلٰهَ غَيْرُكَ

Subḥānak Allāhumma, wa biḥamdika, wa tabārak asmuka, wa Ta'āla jadduka, wa lā ilāha ghayruka.

According to Shāfi`ī *fiqh*:

وَجَّهْتُ وَجْهِيَ لِلَّذِى فَطَرَ ٱلسَّمَٰوَٰتِ وَٱلْأَرْضَ
حَنِيفًا وَمَآ أَنَا۠ مِنَ ٱلْمُشْرِكِينَ ﴿٧٩﴾
إِنَّ صَلَاتِى وَنُسُكِى وَمَحْيَاىَ وَمَمَاتِى لِلَّهِ
رَبِّ ٱلْعَٰلَمِينَ ﴿١٦٢﴾ لَا شَرِيكَ لَهُۥ وَبِذَٰلِكَ أُمِرْتُ وَأَنَا۠ أَوَّلُ ٱلْمُسْلِمِينَ

Wajjahtu wajhīya lilladhī faṭara(a)s-samāwāti wa (a) l` arḍa ḥanīfan wa mā ana min al-mushrikīn; inna Ṣalātī wa nusukī wa maḥyāya wa mamātī lillāhi Rabbi (a)l `Ālamīna lā sharīka-lahu, wa bi dhālika umirtu wa anā awwalu (a)l-Muslimīn.

I have set my face, firmly and truly, towards Him Who created the heavens and the earth, and never shall I make partners with Allāh. Truly, my prayer and my service of sacrifice, my life and my death, are (all) for Allāh, The Cherisher of all the worlds; He has no partners: this am I commanded and I am the first of those who bow to His Will.
(*Al-An'am* 6: 79,162-163)

Following *thana,* the worshiper recites ***Sūrat al-Fātiḥah***

ٱلْحَمْدُ لِلَّهِ رَبِّ ٱلْعَٰلَمِينَ ٱلرَّحْمَٰنِ ٱلرَّحِيمِ مَٰلِكِ يَوْمِ ٱلدِّينِ
إِيَّاكَ نَعْبُدُ وَإِيَّاكَ نَسْتَعِينُ
ٱهْدِنَا ٱلصِّرَٰطَ ٱلْمُسْتَقِيمَ صِرَٰطَ ٱلَّذِينَ أَنْعَمْتَ عَلَيْهِمْ
غَيْرِ ٱلْمَغْضُوبِ عَلَيْهِمْ وَلَا ٱلضَّآلِّينَ

Alḥamdu lillāhi Rabbi (a)l `Ālamīn. Ar-Raḥmāni (a)r-Raḥīm(i). Māliki yawmi (a)d-dīn(i). Iyyāka na'budu,

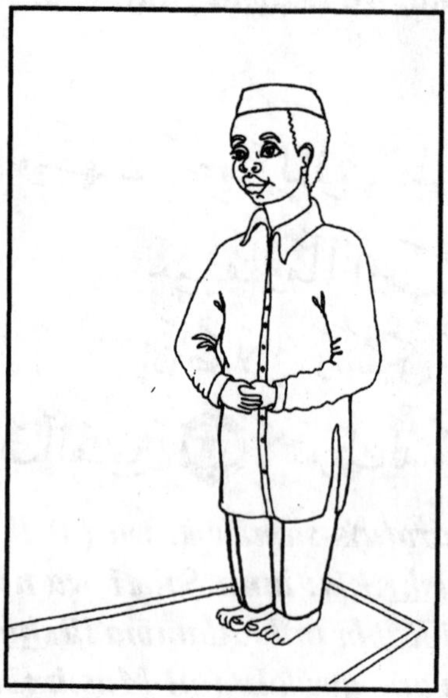

Qiyām: the standing position.

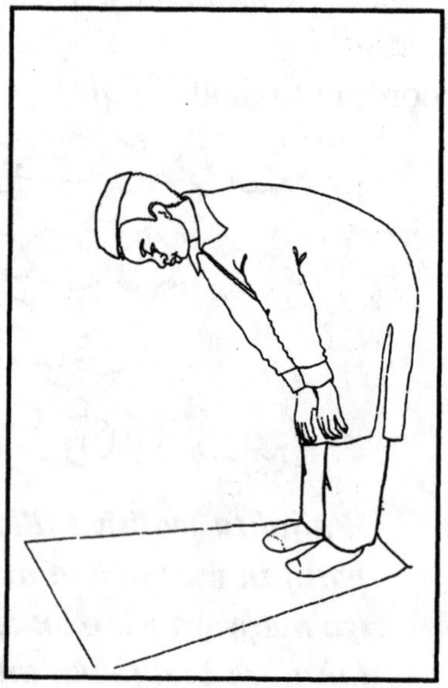

Rukū: the bowing position.

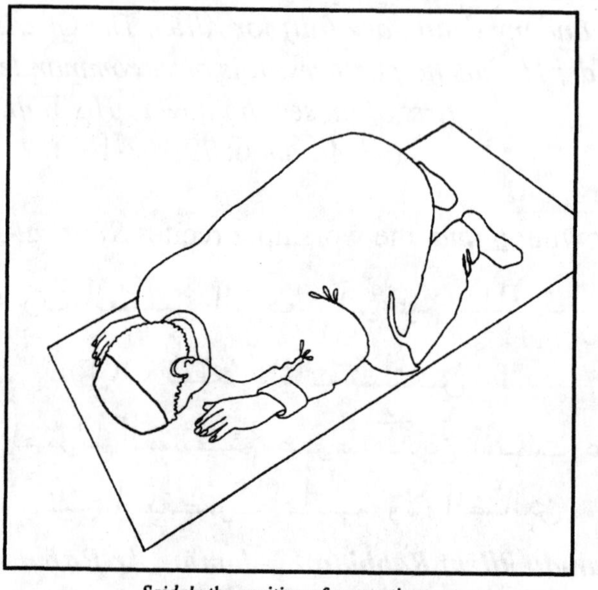

Sajdah: the position of prostration.

wa iyyāka nasta`īn. Ihdina (a)ṣirāṭ al-Mustaqīm. Ṣirāṭ alladh īna `an`amta `alaihim ghairi (a)l maghḍūbi `alaihim. wa la (a)ḍ-ḍāl-līn. Āmīn.

In the name of Allāh, Most Gracious, Most Merciful. All Praise belongs to Allāh, the Sustainer of all the Worlds. Most Gracious, Most Merciful, Lord of the Day of Judgement. You (alone) we worship, and You (alone) we ask for help. Guide us the straight way: The way of those upon whom You have bestowed Your blessings, not of those who earn Your anger, nor of those who go astray. Āmīn.(and then begin the first *Rak'ah.*)

Finally, the worshiper recites another *Sūrah* of the Qur'ān. One may choose to recite one long verse or several relatively short verses of a *Sūrah*. The recitation of a second *Sūrah* after *al-Fātiḥah* is done only in the first two *Raka'āt* of the prayer (if it is a three or four *Raka'āt* prayer). Recitation of *Al-Fātiḥah* and another *Sūrah* should be done aloud or silently, depending on which *Ṣalāh* is being done (see Lesson 15).

Rukū`: The Bowing Position

The worshiper then says: "*Allāhu Akbar*" which means, "Allāh is Most Great!" and bows.

For Shāfi'īs the hands should be raised to shoulder level when saying the *takbīr*. In this position, one should quietly glorify Allāh by saying three times:

سُبْحَانَ رَبِّيَ الْعَظِيْم

Subḥāna Rabbiya (a)l-'Aẓīm.

Glory be to my Sustainer, the Great

سَمِعَ اللّٰهُ لِمَنْ حَمِدَه رَبَّنَا وَلَكَ الْحَمْدُ

Sami' Allāhu li-man ḥamidah, Rab-banā la-kal Ḥamd

He is Allāh, All praise belongs to Allāh.

Shāfi`īs should raise their to shoulder level when coming up from *rukū`*.

Sajdah: Position of Prostration

Again, the worshiper declares: "*Allāhu Akbar,*"moving into prostration, his nose and forehead touching the ground.

Sajdah may be made on any clean material in all the *madhhāhib*.

In this position, one glorifies Allāh ﷻ quietly by repeating the following *taṣbīḥ* three times:

سُبْحَانَ رَبِّيَ الأَعْلَى

Subḥāna Rabbiya (A)l-`A`lā

Glory be to God, the Highest.

Then raise your head from the ground, sitting back, and saying, "*Allāhu Akbar.*" Make a second *Sajdah,* repeating the same *taṣbīḥ*.

Finally, while saying "*Allāhu Akbar,*" rise to the *Qiyām* (standing) position for the second *Rak'ah*.

This completes the first *Rak'ah*. The same procedure is followed for each of the five daily prayers; the only difference is in the intention of the prayer.

✔ EXERCISES

1. Demonstrate the steps of the first *Rak'ah* of prayer.
2. Demonstrate the same steps, and recite out loud what is said during the *Rak'ah*, explaining the meaning of each.

LESSON 14

THE SECOND RAK'AH AND AT-TASHAHHUD

The Same Pattern as the First Rak'ah:

The second *Rak'ah* follows the same pattern as the first *Rak'ah*:

(a) Stand for recitation of *Fātiḥah* and the *Sūrah*.
(One may choose a different *Sūrah* or verses of the Qur'ān this time)
(b) Make *Rukū`* once.
(c) Make two *Sujūd*.

The recitations in all positions are the same as in the first *Rak'ah*.

At-Tashahhud: The Testimony

After the second *Sajdah*, the worshiper raises his head, proclaiming, "*Allāhu Akbar,*" and resumes the sitting position. In this position, he quietly recites *At-Tashahhud* (The Testimony) as follows. According to the Ḥanafī school:

اَلتَّحِيَّاتُ لِلّٰهِ وَٱلصَّلَوٰةُ وَٱلطَّيِّبَاتُ اَلسَّلَامُ عَلَيْكَ اَيُّهَا ٱلنَّبِيُّ

وَرَحْمَةُ ٱللّٰهِ وَبَرَكَاتُهُ ٱلسَّلَامُ عَلَيْنَا وَعَلٰى عِبَادِ ٱللّٰهِ ٱلصَّالِحِيْنَ

أَشْهَدُ أَنْ لَا اِلٰهَ إِلَّا اللّٰهُ وَأَشْهَدُ أَنَّ مُحَمَّدًا عَبْدُهُ وَرَسُوْلُهُ

At-taḥīyyātu li-(A)llāhi wa(a)ṣ-ṣalawātu wa(a)ṭ-ṭayyibātu as-salāmu 'alaika ayyuha (a)n-nabīyyu wa raḥmatu(A)llāhi wa barakātuh(u). As-salāmu 'alainā wa `alā 'ibādi-(A)llāhi(a)ṣ-ṣālihīn*** (raise the index finger of the right hand) ***Ash-hadu an lā ilāha illa- (A)llāh(u)*** (lower the finger) ***wa ash-hadu anna Muḥammadan `abdu-hu wa rasūlu-hū

All greetings, prayers and good things belong to Allāh. O Prophet, peace be upon you and Allāh's Mercy and Blessings. Peace be upon us and on the good servants of Allāh. I bear witness that there is no god but Allāh, and I declare that Muḥammad is His servant and messenger.

According to the Shāfi`ī school, the minimal is:

اَلتَّحِيَّاتُ لِلَّهِ سَلاَمٌ عَلَيْكَ اَيُّهَا النَّبِىُّ
وَرَحْمَةُ اللَّهِ وَبَرَكَاتُهُ سَلاَمٌ عَلَيْنَا وَعَلَى عِبَادِ اللَّهِ الصَّالِحِينَ
اَشْهَدُ أَلاَّ اِلَهَ اِلاَّ اللَّهُ وَاَشْهَدُ اَنَّ مُحَمَّدًا رَسُوْلُ لله

At-taḥīyyātu li-allāhi, salāmun 'alaika ayyuhan nabīyyu wa raḥmatullāhi wa barakātu-hu. Salāmun 'alainā wa `alā 'ibādillāh(a)ṣ-ṣālihīn. Ash-hadu an lā ilāha (raise the index finger of the right hand) ***ila Allāh(ū). Wa ash-ḥadu anna Muḥammadur-Rasūlullāh.***

All greetings to Allāh. Peace be upon you, O Prophet, and the Mercy of Allāh and His Blessings. Peace be to us and on the good servants of Allāh. I bear witness that there is no god but Allāh, and I bear witness that Muḥammad is the Messenger of Allāh.

According to the Mālikī school:

اَلتَّحِيَّاتُ لِلَّهِ اَلزَّاكِيَاتُ لِلَّهِ اَ لطَّيِّبَاتُ وَالصَّلَوَاتُ لِلَّهِ
اَلسَّلاَمُ عَلَيْكَ اَيُّهَا النَّبِىُّ وَرَحْمَةُ اللَّهِ وَبَرَكَاتُهُ
اَلسَّلاَمُ عَلَيْنَا وَعَلَى عِبَادِ اللَّهِ الصَّالِحِينَ
أَشْهَدُ أَلاَّ اِلَهِ اِلاَّ اللَّهُ وَحْدَهُ لا شَرِيكَ لَهُ
وَاَشْهَدُ اَنَّ مُحَمَّدًا عَبْدُهُ وَرَسُوْلُهُ

At-taḥīyyātu lillāhi, Az-zakīyyātu lillāhi, aṭ-ṭayyibātu wa as-Ṣalawātu lillāh. As-salāmu 'alai-ka ayyuha (a)n-nabīyyu wa raḥmatullāhi wa barakātuhu. Assalāmu `alainā wa `alā 'ibādi(A)llāhi (a)ṣ- ṣālihīn. (Index finger of the right hand is raised) ***Ash-hadu an lā ilāha***

illa-(A)llāhu waḥda-hū lā sharīkalahū wa ash-hadu anna Muḥammadan `abdū-hū wa rasūlu-h(ū).

All greetings are for Allāh. All righteousness is for Allāh. All prayers are for Allāh. Peace be upon you, O Prophet, and the Mercy of Allāh and His Blessings. Peace be on us and on the good servants of Allāh. I bear witness that there is no god but Allāh, alone and without partner. And I bear witness that Muḥammad is His servant and messenger.

If *At-Tashahhud* is being recited in the last *Rak'ah* of a prayer (i.e. after the second *Rak'ah* in the *Fajr* Prayer, or the third in the *Maghrib,* or the fourth in all others), one should follow it with *Du'ā' Ibrāhīm,* as follows:

In Ḥanafī, Shāfi'ī, Mālikī and Hanbalī *madhāhib*:

اَللّٰهُمَّ صَلِّ عَلَى مُحَمَّدٍ وَّعَلَى آلِ مُحَمَّدٍ كَمَا صَلَّيْتَ
عَلَى اِبْرَاهِيمَ وَعَلَى آلِ اِبْرَاهِيمَ اِنَّكَ حَمِيدٌ مَجِيدٌ
اَللّٰهُمَّ بَارِكْ عَلَى مُحَمَّدٍ وَعَلَى آلِ مُحَمَّدٍ كَمَا بَارَكْتَ
عَلَى اِبْرَاهِيمَ وَعَلَى آلِ اِبْرَاهِيمَ فِي الْعَالَمِينَ اِنَّكَ حَمِيدٌ مَجِيدٌ.

Allāhumma ṣal-li `alā Muḥammadin wa `alā āli Muḥammadin, Kamā ṣallaita `alā Ibrāhīma wa `alā āli Ibrāhīma Inna-ka Ḥamīdum Majīd. Allāhumma bārik `alā Muḥammadin wa `alā āli Muḥammadin Kamā bārakta `alā Ibrāhīma wa `alā āli Ibrāhīma fi al-`ālamīn. Innaka Ḥamīdum Majīd.

Oh Allāh, send blessings upon Muḥammad and on the family of Muḥammad, as You gave blessings to Ibrāhīm and on the family of Ibrāhīm. You are the Praised, the Most Glorious. O Allāh, bestow grace upon Muḥammad and upon the family of Muḥammad, as You bestowed grace upon Ibrāhīm and upon the family of Ibrāhīm in all worlds. You are the Praised, the Most Glorious.

At-Tashahhud marks the end of the Second *Rak'ah*.

If there are only two *Raka`āt* total in the prayer you are doing, you should end the prayer here as you would if it were a four-*Rak`ah* prayer (see next lesson for details on how prayer is ended).

The Number of Farḍ Raka`āt in Each Daily Prayer

The daily prayers have the following number of *Farḍ Rak`āt*:

1. *Fajr/Ṣubḥ* (dawn): two *Raka`āt*
2. *Ẓuhr* (afternoon): four *Raka`āt*
3. *'Aṣr* (mid-afternoon): four *Raka`āt*
4. *Maghrib* (sunset): three *Raka`āt*
5. *'Ishā'* (twilight): four *Raka`āt*

As you can see, only the *Fajr Ṣalāh* consists of only two *Raka`āt*. For the other four prayers, the worshiper continues to the third *Rak'ah*, which will be described in the next lesson.

✔ EXERCISES

1. Demonstrate the second *Rak'ah* with its steps and its recitations.
2. Recite *At-Tashahhud,* and give its meaning.
3. How many *Raka`āt* are there in each of the five daily prayers?

LESSON 15

THE THIRD AND FOURTH RAKA`ĀT

Rising After At-Tashahhud

Except in *Ṣalāt-al-Fajr* (the Dawn Prayer), one should rise after the first *Tashahhud*, saying *"Allāhu Akbar."*

Reading al-Fātiḥah

The pattern of the third and fourth *Raka'āt* is the same as the first *Rak'ah,* except that there is no other *Sūrah* recited after *al-Fātiḥah.*

Ṣalāt-al-Maghrib

The *Maghrib* prayer consists of three *Raka`āt*. Following the third *Rak'ah,* the worshiper should sit down for *Salām*, recite the full *Tashahhud* and *Du'ā' Ibrāhīm*, and say *As-Salāmu `Alai-kum* to complete his prayer.

Ṣalāt-aẓ-Ẓuhr, 'Aṣr and 'Ishā'

These prayers all consist of four *Raka'āt*. The worshiper must complete four *Raka`āt* and then, while in the sitting position (*Jalsah*), recite the full *Tashahhud* and *Du'ā' Ibrāhīm.* When he says *As-Salāmu `Alai-kum,* he has completed his prayer.

Ending the Ṣalāh

Following the recitation of the *Du'ā' Ibrāhīm*, the worshiper turns his head to the right and says "*As-salāmu `alai-kum wa Raḥmatullāh,*" then turns his head to the left and says "*As-salāmu `alaikum wa Raḥmatullāh.*"

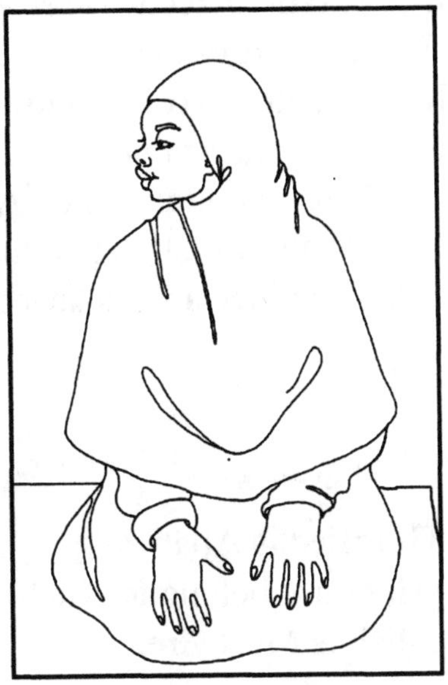

Salām to the left.

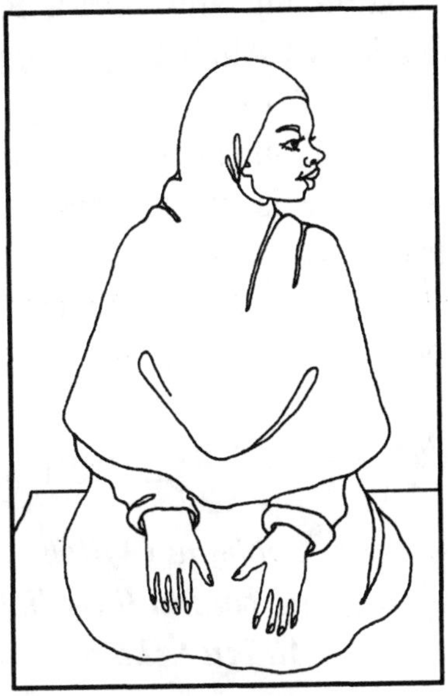

Salām to the right.

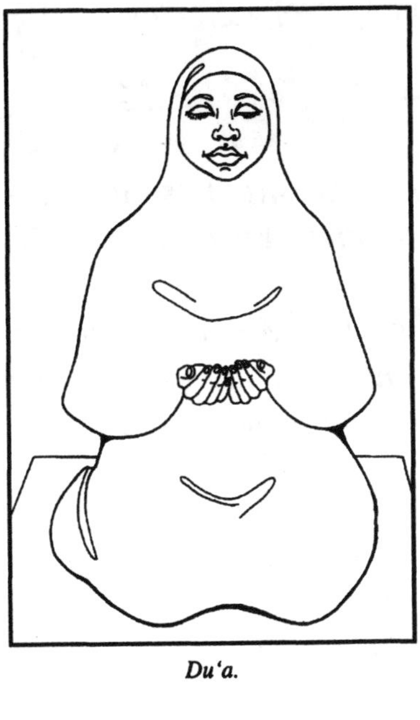

Du'a.

Glorification of Allāh ﷻ:

After completing any *Ṣalāh*, Rasūlullāh ﷺ used to recite *Tasbīḥāt* (the glorification of Allāh ﷻ), *Istighfār* (asking His Forgiveness) and *'Ad`iyā'* (supplications) to Him asking for His Mercy and Favor. Following his *Sunnah,* we should also recite *Tasbīḥāt* and *`Ad`iyā'* in Arabic or in our own language. This is an exercise which helps us focus our attention on Allāh ﷻ and cleanse our mind of distracting thoughts. As the worshiper continues to glorify Allāh ﷻ, he experiences feelings of inner peace and closeness to his Creator.

Tasbīḥāt:

سُبْحَانَ اللّهِ   اَ لحَمْدُ لِلّهِ   اَ للّهُ اكْبَرُ

Subḥana (A)llāh	Glorified is Allāh
Al-ḥamdu li (A)llāh	All praise belong to Allāh
Allāhu 'Akbar	Allāh is Most Great

Each *tasbīḥ* should be repeated a minimum of 33 times. Here is another important *tasbīḥ*:

لآ الِهِ الاّ اللّهُ وَحْدَهُ لا شَرِيكَ لَهُ

لَهُ الْمُلْكُ وَلَهُ الْحَمْدُ وَ هُوَ عَلَي كُلّ شَيْئٍ قَدِيرٍ

Lā ilāha illa (A)llāhu waḥda-hu, lā-sharīka la-h(u) la-hu(a)l-Mulk (u) wa lah(u) (A)l-ḥamd(u) wa Huwa 'alā kulli sha'in Qadīr

There is no God but Allāh, Alone and with no partner. For His is the kingdom, and all praise belongs to Him, and He has power over everything.

***Istaghfār*:**

اَسْتَغْفِرُاللهَ رَبِّي مِنْ كُلِّ ذَنْبٍ وَ اَتُوبُ اِلَيْهِ

Astaghfiru (A)llāha Rabbī min kulli dhanbin wa 'atūbu 'ilai-h(i)

I seek the forgiveness of my Lord from every sin,
and I turn to Him in repentance.

We should always remember to ask Allāh's forgiveness for the sins we are aware of as well as those we may have committed unknowingly. Repeating *Istaghfār*, especially in the morning and before sleeping at night, is said to clear the worshiper of all minor sins committed that day. In fact, Rasūlullāh ﷺ said:

Every one of the children of Adam has been created with 360 joints — so he who . . . seeks forgiveness from Allāh to the number 360 will walk having removed himself from Hell.
(Transmitted by Muslim)

Recitations, Sirrī (Silent) and Jahrī (Out loud):

Women should recite all parts of the prayer silently. An *Imām* should recite the *Fātiḥah* and another *Sūrah* (or part of a *Sūrah*) aloud in the first two *Raka`āt* of the *Fajr, Maghrib,* and *'Ishā'* prayers.

✔ EXERCISES

1. Demonstrate the third and fourth *Raka'āt* with their movements and recitations.
2. Demonstrate with their movements and recitations:
   (a) *Ṣalāt-al-Fajr/Ṣubḥ* (two *Raka'āt*)
   (b) *Ṣalāt-al-Maghrib* (three *Raka'āt*)
   (c) *Ṣalāt-al-'Ishā'* (four *Raka'āt*)

3. In which of the five daily prayers are *al-Fātiḥah* and another *Sūrah* recited silently by all?
4. Explain how *Tasbīḥāt*, *Istaghfār* and *'Ad`iyā'* are done after the ritual *Ṣalāh*.
5. Do women recite anything out loud in any of the prayers?

LESSON 16

THE QUNŪT

The *Qunūṭ* is a special *du'ā* that is recited during the *Witr* or the *Fajr* prayer, depending on the *madhhab*. The word *Qunūt* means "to be obedient."

According to Shāfi 'ī *Fiqh,* the *Qunūt* is recited during *Ṣalāt-al-Fajr*. As the worshiper rises from the *Rukū'* position, he brings his hands to chest level in supplication and says the following:

اَللّهم اهدِ نَا فِي مَن هَدَيتَ وَ عَا فِنا فِي مَنْ عَافَيتَ وَ تَوَلَّنا فِي مَنْ تَوَلَّيتَ
وَ بَارِكْ لَنا فِي مَا أَعْطَيتَ وَ قِنَا شَرَّ مَا قَضَيتَ فَإِنَّكَ تَقْضِي وَ لا يُقْضَي عَلَيْكَ
وَ إِنَّهُ لا يَضِلُّ مَنْ وَالَيتَ تَبا رَكْتَ رَبَّنَا وَتَعَالَيْتَ

Allāhumma(a)hdina fī man hadait, wa `āfin fī man `āfait, wa tawallanī fī man tawallait, wa bārik la-na fi man `a'ṭait, wa qina sharra mā qaḍait, fa inna-ka taqḍī wa lā yuqḍā `alaik. Wa inna-hū lā yaḍillu ma walait, tabārakta Rabbanā wa ta'ālait.

Allāh, guide us amongst those you have guided. Make us healthy among those You have made healthy. Befriend us among those you have befriended. Bless us in what You have given us. Keep away from us the evil that you may have ordained, for surely, You ordain and are not ordained upon and You do not misguide those whom you have befriended and blessed and raised.

According to the Mālikī school, the *Qunūt* is said during *Ṣalāt-al-Fajr* also, but it is recited in the second *rak`ah,* after the recitation of *Fātiḥah* and the second *Sūrah,* just before entering *rukū`*:

اَللّٰهُمَّ اِنَّا نَسْتَعِيْنُكَ وَنَسْتَغْفِرُكَ وَنُؤْمِنُ بِكَ وَنَتَوَكَّلُ عَلَيْكَ

وَنُثْنِى عَلَيْكَ اَلْخَيْرَ نَشْكُرُكَ وَلَا نَكْفُرُكَ وَنَخْلَعُ وَنَتْرُكُ مَنْ يَفْجُرُكَ

اَللّٰهُمَّ اِيَّاكَ نَعْبُدُ وَلَكَ نُصَلِّى وَنَسْجُدُ وَاِلَيْكَ نَسْعٰى

وَنَحْفِدُ نَرْجُوا رَحْمَتَكَ وَنَخْشٰى عَذَابَكَ اِنَّ عَذَابَكَ اَلْجِدَّ بِالْكُفَّارِ مُلْحِق

Oh Allāh, we seek Your help, Your guidance, and Your forgiveness and we believe in You, and we have trust in You, and we praise You in the best way. We thank You, and we do not deny You, And we turn away and give up the friendship of those who disobey You. Oh Allāh, You alone we worship, and for You alone, we offer Ṣalāh, and to You alone, we make sajdah; and we make haste in turning to You, we hope for Your mercy, and we fear Your punishment. Indeed! Your severe punishment overtakes the kuffār.

According to the Ḥanafī *madhhab*, the *Qunūt* is recited only during the *Witr* prayer. The *Qunūt* is recited in the third *rak`ah*, after the *Fātiḥah* and a second *Sūrah* has beeen recited. Then, the hands are raised to the ears, as if making a *takbīr*, and "*Allāhu Akbar*" is said. Having completed this *takbīr*, the hands are returned to their original position, folded across the stomach. Remaining in the standing position, one then recites the *Qunūt*.

اَللّٰهُمَّ اِنَّا نَسْتَعِيْنُكَ وَنَسْتَغْفِرُكَ وَنُؤْمِنُ بِكَ وَنَتَوَكَّلُ عَلَيْكَ

وَنُثْنِى عَلَيْكَ اَلْخَيْرَ وَ نَشْكُرُكَ وَلَا نَكْفُرُكَ وَنَخْلَعُ وَنَتْرُكُ مَنْ يَفْجُرُكَ

اَللّٰهُمَّ اِيَّاكَ نَعْبُدُ وَلَكَ نُصَلِّى وَنَسْجُدُ وَاِلَيْكَ نَسْعٰى

وَنَحْفِدُ نَرْجُوا رَحْمَتَكَ وَنَخْشٰى عَذَابَكَ اِنَّ عَذَابَكَ بِالْكُفَّارِ مُلْحِق

Oh Allāh, we seek Your help, Your guidance, and Your forgiveness and we believe in You, and we have trust in You, and we praise You in the best way. We thank You, and we do not deny You, And we turn away and give up the friendship of those who disobey You. Oh Allāh, You alone we worship, and for You alone, we offer Ṣalāh, and to You alone, we make sajdah; and we make haste in turning to You, we hope for Your mercy, and we fear Your punishment. Indeed! Your severe punishment overtakes the kuffār.

✔ EXERCISES

4. When is the *Qunūt* offered according to Imām Shafi`ī that Shafi`īs recite?
5. Recite the *Qunūt*, you may choose one of the *Qunūt* given in this lesson.
3. When is the *Qunūt* said according to Malikī *Fiqh*?
4. Write the meaning of the *Qunūt* you have memorised.
5. When do Ḥanafīs offer the *Qunūt*?
6. What does a believer promise to Allāh ﷻ in *Qunūt*?

LESSON 17

ṢALĀT-AL-JUMU'AH: THE FRIDAY PRAYER

On Friday, a special *Ṣalāh* is offered in place of *Ṣalāt-aẓ-Ẓuhr*. The worshipers should attend the congregational prayer at the mosques in their cities, towns or localities.

The Khuṭbah

The *Imām* first greets the congregation with a *Khuṭbah* (Sermon), preferably offered in Arabic. However, in areas where Arabic is not spoken, arrangements should be made for translation of the *Khuṭbah* in the local language. The *Khuṭbah* is a very important aspect of *Salāt-al-Jum'ah* and should never be missed.

In his *Khuṭbah*, the *Imām* glorifies Allāh ﷻ and prays for His blessings and mercy on Rasūlullāh ﷺ. He reminds the *jamā'ah* to remember Allāh ﷻ and the teachings of Islām, urging them to do good, and warning them of the pitfalls they may face in contemporary society. Finally, he prays for the congregation and for the entire Muslim *'Ummah.*

The *Imām* then leads the congregation in a prayer consisting of two *Raka'āt*, instead of the usual four *Raka'āt* for the *Ẓuhr* Prayer. He recites out loud, and the congregation follows silently.

The Friday Congregational Prayer is compulsory for men, unless they are on a journey or too ill to attend. It is optional for women (i.e. they may choose to attend or not). If a woman decides to pray at home, or if anyone is prevented from attending *Ṣalāt al-Jumu'ah*, he or she must pray the four *Raka'āt* of the *Ẓuhr* Prayer in the usual manner.

Bath before Friday Prayer

Rasūlullāh ﷺ made it compulsory for everybody who is attending the Friday prayer to bathe before going to the mosque. The bath should be performed in the proper prescribed manner for *Ghusl*. Also, one should dress in one's best clothes. For men, it is recommended to use perfumes (*`Iṭar*).

The Benefits of Ṣalāt al-Jumu'ah

It is narrated by Salmān Farsī ﷺ that the Prophet ﷺ said:

Whoever takes a bath on Friday, purifies himself as much as he can, then uses his (hair) oil or perfumes himself with the scent of his house, then proceeds (for the Jumu'ah prayer) and does not separate two persons sitting together (in the mosque), then prays as much as (Allāh ﷻ has) written for him and then remains silent while the Imām is delivering the Khuṭbah, his sins between the present and the past Friday are forgiven.
(Transmitted by Bukhārī)

Among the many benefits of the *Jumu'ah* prayer, here are just a few:

a. It is an act of obedience to Allāh ﷻ.
b. It brings together all the Muslims of a locality, heightening the spirit of Islāmic brotherhood.
c. The *Khuṭbah* serves as a weekly reminder of our responsibilities as Muslims, warning us of evil and encouraging us to do good.

✔ EXERCISES

1. Where is *Ṣalāt-al-Jumu`ah* offered?
2. What are the differences between *Ṣalāt-al-Jumu`ah* and the *Ẓuhr* Prayers?

3 If someone is not able to go to the *Masjid* for the Friday Prayer, how does he or she pray?

4. What important act of *Sunnah* should a Muslim perform before going to *Ṣalāt-al-Jumu`ah,* and how should it be done?

5. List some of the benefits of *Jumu'ah* Prayer.

LESSON 18

THE COMPULSORY ACTS OF THE ṢALĀH

Categorizing the Acts of Prayer

The acts of prayer may be divided into four types

1. *Farā'iḍ aṣ-Ṣalāh*: compulsory acts of prayer.
2. *Wājibat aṣ-Ṣalāh*: required acts of prayer.
3. *Sunan aṣ-Ṣalāh*: *Sunnah* acts of prayer.
4. *Mustaḥabbāt aṣ-Ṣalāh*: recommended acts of prayer.

It is important to know the differences between these acts of prayer, because in some cases, it may be necessary to repeat or amend the prayer if an omission occurs.

The Farā'iḍ aṣ-Ṣalāh: The Compulsory Acts of Prayer

There are fifteen *Farā'iḍ aṣ-Ṣalāh*:
(**Note**: these are considered the *Wājibāt* in the Ḥanafī *ma<u>dh</u>hab)*

1. Making the intention for the *Ṣalāh.*
2. *Takbīrāt al-Iḥrām*
3. The standing for *Takbīrāt al-Iḥrām*
4. The recitation of *Al-Fātiḥah* in each *Rak'ah*
5. The standing for recitation of *Al-Fātiḥah*
6. Making *Rukū'*
7. *Qawmah*: rising from bowing and standing upright before *Sujūd.*
8. Two *Sujūd*
9. Rising from *Sujūd*
10. *Jalsah*

11. Saying *Salām* to end the prayer
12. *At-Tamaniyyah*: performing the acts of prayer at a steady speed, without rushing
13. Offering the prayer attentively and not in carelessly
14. Performing the *Farā'iḍ aṣ-Ṣalāh* in their correct order
15. When praying behind an *Imām,* making the intention to follow the *Imām* in prayer.

To these, must be added the following:

1. Cleanliness of body
2. Cleanliness of clothes
3. Cleanliness of place
4. Covering the *Satr*
5. Facing the *Qiblah*
6. Praying at the appointed time
7. Intention of the *Ṣalāh*

Omission of a Farḍ Act of Prayer

Case I: If a person unintentionally omits a *Farḍ* act of the *Ṣalāh*, but remembers it before he rises from *Sujūd* in the next *Rak'ah*, he must go back to the act omitted and complete the *Ṣalāh* properly from that act to the end. After "*Assalāmu 'Alai-kum wa raḥmatullāh,*" he should perform *Ba'dī,* two prostrations of amendment (see Lesson 22). According to the Ḥanafī school, the entire prayer must be repeated, and the *Sajdah Sahw* (see Lesson 22) will not suffice.

Case II. If a person unintentionally omits a *Farḍ* act of the *Ṣalāh,* but remembers it after he rises from *Sajdah* in the next *Rak'ah*, he should discard the *Rak'ah* in which he made the error and substitute it with the *Rak'ah* he is now in. He should then complete the remaining *Raka'āt* of the prayer.
After "*Assalāmu 'Alai-kum wa raḥmatullāh,*" he should perform two *Sujūd of Sahw* (see Lesson 22).

Case III. If a person unintentionally omits a *Farḍ* act of the *Ṣalāh* and does not remember it until after finishing the *Ṣalāh*, he should repeat the whole *Ṣalāh*.

✔ EXERCISES

1. Why is it important to know the difference between the *Farḍ*, *Sunnah* and recommended acts of the *Ṣalāh*?
2. What are the *Farā'iḍ aṣ-Ṣalāh*?
3. Describe how to amend the *Ṣalāh* if a *Farḍ* act is omitted.

LESSON 19

THE SUNNAH ACTS OF THE ṢALĀH

The Sunan aṣ-Ṣalāh

Rasūlullāh ﷺ initiated the following acts of the *Ṣalāh.* Therefore, it is important to include them in the *Ṣalāh.* Of these, eight are considered to be especially important (marked with an *):

1.* The recitation of a *Sūrah* or verse of the Qur'ān after *al-Fātiḥah* in the first two *Raka'āt* of every *Farḍ Ṣalāh.*

2. The *Qiyyām* (standing position) for the recitation of the Qur'ān after *al-Fātiḥah.*

3.* The recitation of *al-Fātiḥah* and another *Sūrah* out loud, where it is recommended (i.e. in the first two *Raka'āt* of *Fajr/Ṣubh, Maghrib* and *'Ishā' Ṣalāt* and Friday *Ṣalāh*).

4.* The recitation of *al-Fātiḥah* and another *Sūrah* silently, where it is recommended (i.e. all *Raka'āt* of *Farḍ,* except those mentioned in #3 above).

5.* The saying of *"Allāhu 'Akbar"* on each occasion in the *Ṣalāh*, except the first *Takbirāt-al-Iḥrām*, which is *Farḍ.*

6.* To say "*Sami'a (A)llāhu li-man ḥamidah(u)*" (which means: "Allāh hears him who praises Him") each time when rising from *Rukū`*.

7.* To recite the first *Tashahhud (At-Taḥiyyāt)* after the second

Rak'ah of the prayers that consists of more than two *Rak'āt*.

8.* The sitting position for the first *Tashahhud (At-Taḥiyyāt)*

9.* To recite the second *Tashahhud* at the end of the last *Rak'ah* of each *Ṣalāh*.

10. The sitting position for recitation of the second *Tashahhud.*

11. To ask for the blessings of Allāh ﷻ on Prophet Muḥammad ﷺ at the end of the final *Tashahhud* before saying, *"Assalāmu 'Alai-kum wa raḥmatu(A)llāh."* (The recommended form of saying this is given in Lesson 14)

12. When making *Sajdah,* the worshiper should rest his weight on his hands, knees and toes, not on his elbows or forearms.

13. After saying the final *"Assalāmu 'Alai-kum wa raḥmatullāh"* to the right, the follower of the *Imām* should say *"Assālamu 'Alai-kum"* towards the *Imām* and towards any person who is sitting to his left.

14. To say the compulsory *"Assalāmu 'Alai-kum wa raḥmatu(A)llāh"* out loud at the end of the *Ṣalāh.*

15. To follow the *Imām's* recitation attentively.

16. To show great patience in performing the acts of the *Ṣalāh.*

Omission of a Sunnah Act of Ṣalāh

Case I. If a person omits any of the especially important *Sunnah* acts of *Ṣalāh* (marked by * in the list above), he should perform two *Sujūd as-Sahw*, prostrations of amendment, before finishing his *Ṣalāh* with: *"Assalāmu 'Alai-*

kum wa raḥmatu(A)llāh" (i.e. *Sujūd al-Qāblī*, see Lesson 22).

Case II. If a person omits only one of the other *Sunnah* acts of *Ṣalāh*, he should not amend the *Ṣalāh*. By doing so, he would nullify his *Ṣalāh*.

Case III. However, if he omits two of the less important acts of the *Ṣalāh*, he should perform two *Sujūd as-Sahw* before finishing his *Ṣalāh* with: "*Assalāmu 'Alai-kum wa raḥmatullāh*" (i.e. *Sujūd al-Qāblī*, see Lesson 22).

✔ EXERCISES

1. List the *Sunnah* acts of *Ṣalāh*.
2. Which eight of the *Sunnah* acts of the *Ṣalāh* are considered especially important?
3. Recite the short *du'ā* for blessing on Prophet Muḥammad ﷺ which is recited after the second *Tashahhud*, and give its meaning.
4. What would you do if you omitted:
   (a) one of the eight more important acts of *Sunan* of the *Ṣalāh*?
   (b) one of the less important acts of *Sunan aṣ-Ṣalāh*?
   (c) two of the less important acts of *Sunan aṣ-Ṣalāh*?

LESSON 20

MERITORIOUS ACTS OF ṢALĀH

The Mustaḥabbāt aṣ-Ṣalāh

There are over thirty *Mustaḥabbāt aṣ-Ṣalāh* (recommended acts of *Ṣalāh*). Six examples are given here:

1. To look at the place of *Sujūd* for the duration of the *Ṣalāh*.

2. To form straight rows when praying in a *jamā'ah. jamā`h.*

3. The recitation of the *Qunūt* (see Lesson 16) before *Rukū'* in the second *Rak'ah* of the *Fajr Ṣalāh*.

4. To recite: *"Rabbanā wa la-ka al-ḥamd",* which means: "Our Lord, all praise belongs to You" after reciting: "*Sami` Allāhu li-man ḥamidah*" when rising from *Rukū`*.

5. To raise the hand during the *Takbīrāt al-Iḥrām* (the first "*Allāhu Akbar*").

6. To say "*Āmīn*" after recitation of *al-Fātiḥah*.

Omission of any of these acts does not nullify the *Ṣalāh,* and no amendment is required. However, inclusion of these acts greatly merits and benefits the worshiper.

✔ EXERCISES

1. Name six of the recommended acts of *Ṣalāh*.
2. Does omission of any of the *Mustaḥabbāt aṣ-Ṣalāh* nullify the *Ṣalāh*?

LESSON 21

CONDITIONS THAT NULLIFY THE ṢALĀH

A number of conditions may nullify the *Ṣalāh*. Some of the most important ones to remember are:

1. Anything which nullifies the *Wuḍū'* nullifies the *Ṣalāh*
2. Talking or laughing during the prayer
3. Eating or drinking anything while praying
4. Interrupting the *Ṣalāh* for some other activity (except for a minor interruption in the interest of safety or saving your life).
5. Uncovering the private parts
6. Intentionally turning away from the *Qiblah* completely
7. Omission of a *Farḍ* or an important *Sunnah* act of the *Ṣalāh* (unless amended as described in Lessons 18, 19 and 22)

The *Ṣalāh* which is nullified by any of these circumstances must be repeated.

What to Avoid in Ṣalāh

It is highly undesirable for someone to be inattentive during the *Ṣalāh*. According to a *Ḥadīth* from Abu Dhar ﷺ, related by Abū Dā'ūd and Nisā'ī, Rasūlullāh ﷺ said that Allāh ﷻ does not attend to the *Ṣalāh* of someone who offers it without paying attention. Abū Hurairah ﷺ also reported Rasūlullāh ﷺ as saying: "Call upon Allāh ﷻ being certain of His response, and know that Allāh ﷻ does not respond to the call of a negligent and careless heart." (Tirmi<u>dh</u>ī) Therefore, it is important to avoid anything that may cause your thoughts to wander during the *Ṣalāh*.

✔ EXERCISES

1. Name seven things which nullify the *Ṣalāh*.
2. If a *Ṣalāh* is nullified, what should the worshiper do?
3. If one passes wind while he is praying, what should he do?
4. If someone talks to you while you are praying, what should you do?
5. Explain why paying attention during *Ṣalāh* is very important.

LESSON 22

SAJDAH SAHW: AMENDING ṢALĀH BY PROSTRATION

Sujūd Al-Qāblī

If a worshiper omits one of the eight necessary *Sunnah* acts of the *Ṣalāh* (see Lesson 19) in a *Farḍ Ṣalāh,* he should amend his *Ṣalāh* by making two *Sujūd* of amendment before saying, *"Assalāmu 'Alai-kum wa raḥmatu(A)llāh."* This is called *Sujūd al-Qāblī.*

Following is the proper procedure to perform *Sujūd al-Qāblī*

1. After reciting *At-Tashahhud*, remain seated.
2. Prostrate, saying: *"Allāhu 'Akbar."*
3. Raise your head, saying: *"Allāhu 'Akbar"* and return to the sitting position.
4. Repeat the prostration with the same recitation. Once again, return to the sitting position.
5. Recite *At-Tashahhud* again.
6. End the *Ṣalāh* with *"Assalāmu 'Alai-kum wa raḥmatu(A)llāh."*

If the worshiper forgets to do *Sujūd al-Qāblī* before *Salām*, he can do it after. In this case, he should first make the intention to offer *Ṣalāh*.

However, if he leaves the place of worship before he remembers the omission, it is too late to amend it. The *Ṣalāh* is considered void, and he should repeat it in its entirety.

It must be understood that *Sujūd al-Qāblī* should not be done for omission of just one of the less important *Sunnah* acts of *Ṣalāh*, nor for the *Mustaḥab* acts of *Ṣalāh*. If the worshiper performs *Sujūd al-Qāblī* when it is not required, the *Ṣalāh* is nullified and should be repeated. This is why it is so important to know the different categories of the acts of *Ṣalāh*.

Sujūd al-Ba'dī

According to *Maliki Fiqh*, if one of the following are repeated by mistake: (a) a *Farḍ* act of *Ṣalāh*; (b) an important *Sunnah* act of *Ṣalāh;* or (c) two or more of the less important *Sunnah* acts of *Ṣalāh*, one should amend his *Ṣalāh* by two prostrations after *Salām*. This is called *Sujūd al-Ba'dī*. Following is the proper procedure to perform *Sujūd al-Ba'dī:*

1. After finishing the *Ṣalāh* with "*Assalāmu 'Alai-kum,*" remain seated.
2. Silently, make the intention to perform *Sujūd al-Ba'dī* for the amendment of *Ṣalāh*.
3. Perform the prostrations in the manner described above in #2 through #5 of *Sujūd al-Qāblī*.

Sujūd al-Ba'dī may be offered whenever the mistake is realized: after leaving the place of worship, the next day, or even a year later.

✔ EXERCISES

1. What is *Sujūd al-Qāblī*?
2. How is *Sujūd al-Qāblī* performed? Explain and demonstrate.
3. What kind of mistake makes *Sujūd al-Qāblī* necessary?
4. What should one do if he forgets to do *Sujūd al-Qāblī* at its proper time, before ending with: "*Assalāmu 'Alai-kum*"?
5. What is *Sujūd al-Ba'dī*?
6. How is *Sujūd al-Ba'dī* performed? Explain and demonstrate.
7. What would a person do if he forgets to do *Sujūd al-Ba'dī* until after leaving the place of worship?

LESSON 23

PRAYING BEHIND AN IMĀM

The Standing Order of the Congregation

The *Imām* is the one who leads others in *Ṣalāh*. He should stand in front. The position of the followers will depend on their number, and whether they are male or female.

The following chart shows how the positions of the *Imām* and followers vary according to each situation. (Note: the position of the *Imām* is represented by the ▲ symbol, while males are represented by ■ symbols, and females are represented by ● symbols.)

QIBLAH		
▲■	▲ ●	▲■ ●
Imām + 1 male	*Imām* + 1 female	*Imām* + 1 male + 1 female
▲ ●●	▲■ ●●	▲ ■■■ ●●●
Imām + 2 female	*Imām* + 1 male +2 females	*Imām* + 3 male +3 females

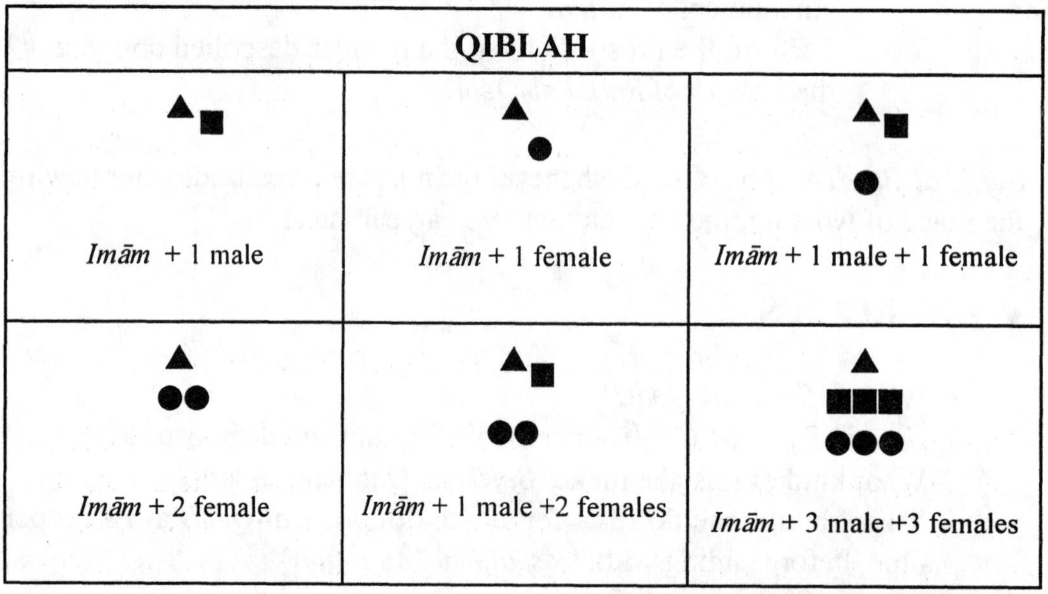

If there are many followers, they can form rows. However, the front rows should be filled first, leaving no gaps. The worshipers should stand shoulder-to-shoulder in straight rows. Females rows should begin behind the males.

Giving the 'Iqāmah

One of the worshipers will give the *'Iqāmah* (i.e. the call to start the *Ṣalāh*) out loud, and the *Ṣalāh* will begin.

Intention to Follow the Imām

The followers should indicate in their intention that they are going to follow an *Imām* in *Ṣalāh.*

Following the Reading Silently

When the *Imām* recites from the Qur'ān out loud, the other worshipers should follow the words silently. When the *Imām* recites from the Qur'ān silently, the other worshipers may also recite silently (i.e. *Fātiḥah* and any other *Sūrah* they may choose). Similarly, *At-Tashahhud* should be read silently by both the *Imām* and the followers.

Assalāmu 'Alai-kum wa Raḥmatu(A)llāh

The *Imām* ends his *Ṣalāh* saying, "*Assalāmu 'Alai-kum wa raḥmatu(A)llāh*" out loud, turning his head to the right. The followers do the same, saying "*Assalāmu 'Alai-kum*" silently towards the *Imām* and again to anyone who may be praying to their left. It is also correct for both the *Imām* and the followers to say "*Assalāmu 'Alai-kum wa raḥmatu(A)llāh*" to the right and left.

Here, we see the *Jamā'ah* at Jāma' Masjid in New Delhi, India. This is the largest mosque in India and the second largest mosque in the world.

One Must Not Go Ahead of the Imām

The followers must offer the movements of the *Ṣalāh* after the *Imām*, and not race ahead of him. In particular, if any follower begins the *Ṣalāh* with *"Allāhu 'Akbar"* before the *Imām,* or says his final *"Assalāmu 'Alai-kum wa rahmatullāh"* before the *Imām*, that person's *Ṣalāh* becomes void and should be repeated.

Maturity of an Imām

An *Imām* should have reached the age of maturity, if he is to lead other adults in *Ṣalāh*. The age of maturity is marked by the onset of puberty.

✔ EXERCISES

1. Explain or demonstrate how the following groups should stand for *Ṣalāh*:
   (a) The *Imām* and one male follower
   (b) The *Imām* and one female follower
   (c) The *Imām*, one male, and one female follower
   (d) The *Imām*, and two female followers
   (e) The *Imām*, one male, and two female followers
   (f) The *Imām*, three male, and three female followers.
2. How would you make intention of *Ṣalāh* when following an *Imām*?
3. How should the *Imām* say the final *Assalāmu 'Alai-kum* of *Ṣalāh*?
4. How should the followers of an *Imām* say the final *Assalāmu 'Alai-kum* of *Ṣalāh*?
5. If a follower says the final *"Assalāmu 'Alai-kum"* before the *Imām*, what is the result?
6. Can a child lead an adult in *Ṣalāh*?
7. The following chart shows at least four mistakes in standing for *Ṣalāh* with an *Imām*. Spot the mistakes, and show how the people should stand correctly. (Note: the position of the *Imām* is represented by the ▲ symbol, while males are represented by ■ symbols, and females are

represented by ● symbols.)

QIBLAH	
a) ▲■ *Imām* + 1 male	b) ▲ ● *Imām* + 1 female
c) ▲■ ●● *Imām* + 1 male +2 females	▲ ■　　■ ●●●■ *Imām* + 3 male +3 females

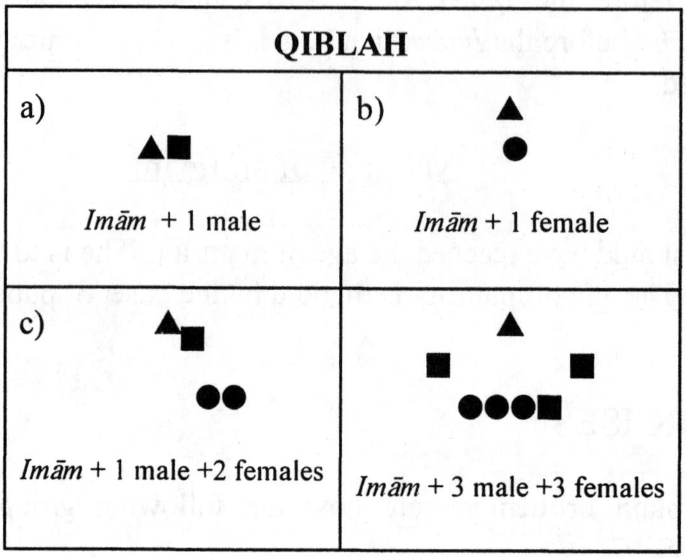

LESSON 24

THE ṢALĀH OF THE LATECOMER AND QAḌĀ'

When is a Latecomer in Time to Join the Imām?

If the *Imām* has already started the *Ṣalāh*, a latecomer can still join and complete the remainder of the prayer in *jamā'ah.* He can then complete the missed portion after the *Imām* has finished. However, if the latecomer joins the *Imām* after he has completed the *Rukū`* of the last *Rak'ah*, the latecomer should offer the entire *Ṣalāh* individually, after the *Imām* finishes leading the prayer.

How to Join the Ṣalāh

The latecomer should take his place, steady himself, make the intention to follow the *Imām* in the *Ṣalāh* concerned, and do the *Takbirāt al-Iḥrām.* He then joins in the *Ṣalāh,* following the *Imām* at whatever stage of the *Ṣalāh* he may be.

If he joins a *Rak'ah* before the *Imām* rises from the *Rukū ',* he should count that *Rak'ah* as his first. However, if the *Imām* has already completed the *Rukū'*, he should not count this *Rak'ah* as his first. Instead, he should begin counting from the next *Rak'ah.*

Missing the First Rak`ah of the Ṣalāh

If the latecomer has missed only the first *Rak'ah* with the *Imām,* he should not participate in the final "*Assalāmu 'Alai-kum wa raḥmatu(A)llāh*" with the *jamā'ah.* Instead, he should rise and complete the first *Rak`ah* that he missed (with *al-Fātiḥah* and another *Sūrah*, recited out loud or silently, depending on the *Ṣalāh*) then sit for *Tashahhud* and end his *Ṣalāh* with *Assalāmu 'Alai-kum* *wa raḥmatu(A)llāh.*

Missing the First Two Raka'āt of a Four-Raka`āt Ṣalāh

In this case, the latecomer completes the third and fourth *Raka'āt* with the *Imām*. When the *Imām* ends his *Ṣalāh*, the latecomer should not say "*Assalāmu 'Alai-kum wa raḥmatu(A)llāh.*" Instead, he should stand up, saying, *Allāhu Akbar*, and offer the first and second *Raka`āt* that he missed, including *al-Fātihah* and another *Sūrah*. Then, he should sit for *at-Tashahhud* and end his *Ṣalāh* with "*Assalāmu 'Alai-kum wa raḥmatu(A)llāh.*"

Missing the First Three of a Four-Raka'āt Ṣalāh

In the case of a four-*Raka`āt Ṣalāh* (*Ẓuhr, 'Aṣr* or *`Ishā'*), the latecomer completes only the fourth *Rak'ah* with the *Imām*. When the *Imām* says, "*Assalāmu 'Alai-kum wa raḥmatu(A)llāh,*" the latecomer stands up and offers the first *Rak'ah* with the *al-Fātiḥah* and another *Sūrah* and the third *Rak'ah* (reciting the *Fātiḥah* only). He should then complete the *Ṣalāh* with *at-Tashahhud* and *Du'ā' Ibrāhīm*, finishing with *Salām* to the right and left shoulders (in that order).

Missing the First Two Rak'āt of a Three-Raka'āt Ṣalāh

Now, let us consider the case of the three-*Raka`āt Ṣalāh* (the *Maghrib Ṣalāh).* Having missed the first two *Raka'āt*, the latecomer can only offer one *Rak'ah* (number three) with the *Imām*. When the *Imām* says *Salām* to end the prayer, the latecomer does not follow the *Imām*. Instead, he stands up and offers the first *Rak'ah* (with *al-Fātiḥah* and another *Sūrah*). Since, he has now completed two *Raka'āt* (number three and one), he should sit for *Tashahhud*. Following this, he should stand up for the second missed *Rak'ah* (number two with *Al-Fātiḥah* and another *Sūrah*) and continue with *Tashahhud* and *Du'ā' Ibrāhīm (Darud* or *Salat Ibrahimiyyah),* completing his *Ṣalāh* with *Salām* to the right and left shoulders.

<u>Making Up the Missed Ṣalāh</u>

If a person has missed one or more prayer, he must make it (them) up as soon as he is able to do so. This kind of *Ṣalāh* is called *Qaḍā'*. When praying *Qaḍā'*, he must mention in his intention the name of the *Ṣalāh* he is making up.

If a person misses fewer than five *Ṣalāwāt*, he should complete them in their correct order before the next due *Ṣalāh*. If he misses more than five *Ṣalawāt*, he should pray the currently due *Ṣalāh* first, and then make up the missed *Ṣalawāt* in their correct order.

One can make up a *Ṣalāh* at any time of the day or night. The missed *Ṣalawāt* do not have to be made up at their respective correct times. However, since they are already overdue, they should be made up as soon as possible.

✔ EXERCISES

1. A latecomer has missed a *Rak'ah* if he joins *Ṣalāh* after the *Imām* has _________ (complete the sentence).
2. When the latecomer joins the *Ṣalāh* behind an *Imām* what should he do?
3. Describe or demonstrate how to complete the *Ṣalāh* if you have:
   (a) missed the first *Rak'ah* of any *Ṣalāh*
   (b) missed the first two *Raka'āt* of a four-*Raka'āt* *Ṣalāh*
   (c) missed the first three *Raka'āt* of a four- *Raka'āt* *Ṣalāh*
4. A person was prevented from praying his *Fajr, Ẓuhr, 'Aṣr* and *Maghrib* *Ṣalāwāt* at their appointed times. It is now time for *Ṣalāt al-`Ishā'*. In which order should he make up his missed prayers?
5. A person was prevented from praying all his five ritual *Ṣalāwāt* for one day, and also his *Fajr Ṣalāh* the following morning. It is now time for *Ṣalāt al-Ẓuhr*. In which order will he make up the missed prayers?

LESSON 25

ṢALĀH UNDER SPECIAL CIRCUMSTANCES

A Sick Person's Ṣalāh

If a person is well enough to stand for *Ṣalāh*, he should do so. If he cannot stand, he may pray sitting. If that is not possible, he may pray lying on his right side. If all movement is impossible, he may pray in his heart, and move his eyes to indicate when he would bow or prostrate. Thus, unless a person is actually unconscious or mentally incapable, he is required to offer *Ṣalāh* in any manner possible.

Qaṣr Ṣalāh: Praying on a Journey

It is an important *Sunnah* that a traveler offer the *Qaṣr* (shortened)*Ṣalāh*. The prayers that may be shortened are the four-*Raka`āt Ṣalāwāt* (*Ẓuhr, 'Aṣr and 'Ishā'*). The *Fajr* and *Maghrib Ṣalāwāt* cannot be shortened. The traveler makes the intention of shortening the *Ṣalāh* and prays the first two *Raka'āt* only, then recites the *Tashahhud* and ends his *Ṣalāh* with *Salām* to the right and left shoulders.

However, if the traveler prays behind an *Imām* who is not a traveler, he should complete the full *Ṣalāh* of four *Raka`āt*. If the *Imām* is the traveler, he should pray only two *Rak`āt* and any residents who follow him should then rise after *Tashahhud* and complete their *Ṣalāh* as usual.

To qualify for *Qaṣr Ṣalāh,* all of the following conditions must apply:

(a) The journey should be to a place at least 77 kilometers (48 miles) distant;
(b) The journey should not be for an illegal purpose (e.g. to commit a crime);

(c) The traveler should have already started his journey; and must be away from his city, town, or village.

Jam'ah bain aṣ-Ṣalātain: Combining Two Ṣalawāt

It is also permissible to combine two *Ṣalawāt* at one time on a journey: *Ẓuhr* and *'Aṣr* may be combined and *Maghrib* and *'Ishā'* may be combined. (According to the Ḥanafī School, *Qaṣr Ṣalawāt* is not allowed to be combined and each prayer must be offered at its appointed time.)

The combined *Ṣalāh* may be done either 'in advance' or 'in delay.' When it is 'in advance,' *'Aṣr* is brought forward to the time of *Ẓuhr*, and *'Ishā'* is brought forward to the time of *Maghrib*. When it is 'in delay,' *Ẓuhr* is delayed until the time of *Aṣr*, and *Maghrib* is delayed until the time of *'Ishā'*.

This permission to combine the *Ṣalāh* is very useful on a long journey, since it is not always possible to stop at the appointed time. It also reduces delays and minimizes the possibility of danger during a stop.

✔ EXERCISES

1. What is *Qaṣr Ṣalāh?* How should the *Qaṣr Ṣalāh* be offered?
2. If a traveler prays behind a resident *Imām,* should the traveler shorten his *Ṣalāh*?
3. If a traveler is the *Imām* for resident followers, should he shorten his *Ṣalāh*? Should the followers who are residents also shorten their *Ṣalāh*?
4. What are the conditions for shortening the *Ṣalāh* on a journey?
5. What does *Jam'ah baina Ṣalātain* mean?
6. Which *Ṣalawāt* may be combined by a traveler?
7. What is the meaning of 'in advance' and 'in delay' when combining *Ṣalāh*?
8. How does combining the *Ṣalāh* help a traveler?

LESSON 26

SUPEREROGATORY ṢALĀH: THE NAWĀFIL

The Purpose of Salawāt an-Nawāfil

The *Nawāfil* prayers are strongly recommended for extra benefit and reward to the worshiper. Some such prayers may be offered daily, just before or just after the *Farḍ Ṣalāh*. Others are offered on special occasions and will be discussed in the next lesson.

How to Offer the Ṣalawāt-an-Nawāfil

No *'Iqāmah* is required for the *Nawāfil Ṣalawāt*. The worshiper makes the intention for *Nafl Ṣalāh* and prays as usual. The *Nawāfil Ṣalawāt* occur in pairs of two *Raka`āt* each. Thus, if four *Raka`āt* are recommended, they should be done in pairs two *Raka`āt,* each with a separate intention, each beginning with its respective *Takbirāt-al-Iḥrām* and ending with *Salām*.

The only exception is the last prayer of the night (*Witr*) which comprises only one *Rak'ah*.

Mistakes in The Nawāfil Ṣalāh

If a mistake is made in the *Nafl* prayer, it may be amended by *Sajdah Sahw* (*Qāblī* or *Ba'dī,* as applicable).

The Nawāfil Ṣalawāt for a Traveler

It is not desirable for a traveler who is shortening his *Ṣalāh* (see Lesson 26) to offer the *Nawāfil Ṣalawāt* except for Shafa', *Witr Ṣalāh,* and the two *Raka`āt* before *Ṣalāt al-Fajr*.

The following table shows the recommended *Nawāfil Ṣalawāt*

PRAYER	NAWAFIL	BEFORE OR AFTER FARḌ	SILENTLY OR OUT LOUD	RECITE
Ṣalāt ul-Fajr	Two *Raka'āt*	Before	Silently	*Fātihah & Sūrah*
Ṣalāt ul-Zuhr	Four *Raka'āt*	Before & After	Both Silently	*Fātihah & Sūrah*
Ṣalāt ul-'Asr	Four *Raka'āt*	Before	Silently	*Fātihah & Sūrah*
Ṣalāt ul-Maghrib	Two *Raka'āt*	After	Silently or out loud	*Fātihah & Sūrah*
Ṣalāt-ul-'Isha	Two *Raka'āt*	After	Silently or out loud	*Fātihah & Sūrah*

Times When the Nawāfil Ṣalawāt Should Not Be Offered

There are certain instances in which it is undesirable to offer *Nawāfil Ṣalawāt*. One should avoid the following times:

1. At sunrise.
2. At sunset.
3. During the *Khuṭbah* (Sermon) of *Salāt al-Jumu'ah*, (the Friday Prayer).
4. Before offering *Qaḍā'* for a missed *Farḍ Ṣalāh*.

The Rewards of the Nawāfil Ṣalawāt

The Muslim who wishes to draw closer to Allāh ﷻ will experience the benefits and rewards of offering these extra prayers. Abū Hurairah ؓ reported from Rasūlullāh ﷺ reported that Allāh ﷻ said:

So often does My servant draw near to Me with the Nawāfil acts of worship, until I love him. And if I love him, I will be his hearing with which he hears, his sight with which he sees, and his hands with which he holds, and his legs with which he walks. If he asks for something, I shall grant it. If he seeks refuge, I shall grant him refuge.
(Al-Bukhārī)

✔ EXERCISES

1. Is there any *'Iqāmah* for the *Nawāfil Ṣalawāt*?
2 Describe the *Nawāfil Ṣalawāt* recommended with each of the five daily ritual prayers.
3 Is it desirable for a traveler to offer the *Nawāfil Ṣalawāt*? Why or why not?
4 Are prostrations of *Qāblī* or *Ba'dī* offered to amend a mistake in a the *Nawāfil Ṣalawāt*?
5 Name four occasions when the *Nawāfil Ṣalawāt* should not be offered.
6 What sort of benefit can a Muslim expect from doing the *Nawāfil Ṣalawāt* in light of a *Ḥadīth* narrated by Abū Hurairah ﷺ?

LESSON 27

EXAMPLES OF THE NAWĀFIL ṢALĀH

Ṣalāt-at-Tahajjud or Qiyām al-Lail

It was a tradition of Rasūlullāh ﷺ and his *Ṣaḥābah* ﷺ to offer the *Ṣalāt-at-Tahajjud*. This is a late night *Nawāfil Ṣalāh* to be offered regularly, as recommended in the Qur'ān:

وَمِنَ ٱلَّيۡلِ فَتَهَجَّدۡ بِهِۦ
نَافِلَةٗ لَّكَ عَسَىٰٓ أَن يَبۡعَثَكَ رَبُّكَ مَقَامٗا مَّحۡمُودٗا ﴿٧٩﴾

Besides this, offer Tahajjud prayer: it may be that your Lord will raise you to a praised position.
(*Sūrah Isrā'* 17: 79)

The preferred time for *Ṣalāt-at-Tahajjud* is during the last third of the night before dawn. However, it can be offered in any part of the night.

It was Rasūlullāh's habit to offer twelve *Raka`āt* including *Shafa'* (i.e. six pairs) and end with the single *Rak'ah* of *Witr*. (According to the Ḥanafī school, the two *Nawāfil* of *Shafa'* are combined with the one *Witr Rak'ah*). One may do any number of pairs of *Raka`āt* with a minimum of one pair.

If a person has already prayed two *Raka`āt* of *Shafa'* and one *Rak`ah* of *Witr* after the *'Ishā'* prayer in the early part of the night, there is no need to repeat them.

Ṣalāt at-Tarāwīḥ During Ramaḍān

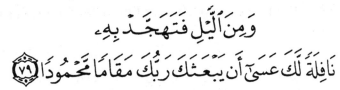

During the month of Ramaḍān, the *Nawāfil Ṣalawāt* of *Tahajjud* is offered in the earlier part of the night after *'Ishā' Ṣalāh*, and is called *Tarāwīḥ*.

As in *Tahajjud*, the *Ṣalāh* consists of a total of thirteen *Raka`āt* (six pairs including *Shafa'* and ending with the single *Rak'ah* of *Witr*). Some people increase the number to twenty *Raka`āt* plus three *Witr*, which is also good. Rasūlullāh ﷺ offered *Tarāwīḥ* in many ways, all of which are acceptable.

The *Tarāwīḥ* is generally offered in *Jamā`ah* led by an *Imām* who is a *Ḥāfiẓ* (one who has memorized the Qur'ān). Each night, the *Ḥāfiẓ* recites a portion of the Qur'ān, completing the entire recitation on any of the last ten odd nights of Ramaḍān. A person may also offer the *Tarāwīḥ* at home, individually or with the family, reciting all the portions of the Qur'ān one remembers.

Ṣalāt al-Janāzah: the Funeral Ṣalāh

Ṣalāt-al-Janāzah for the dead Muslim brother or sister is a *Farḍ Kifāyah* incumbent on every Muslim. *Farḍ Kifāyah* is a religious obligation required of every Muslim in a community; however, if even a few members of the community fulfill it, the obligation is fulfilled for all the Muslims of the community. If no one completes the obligation, then every Muslim in the community is accountable for it.

When a Muslim dies, adult or child, the body is washed as for *Wuḍū'* and Expiation. It is then wrapped in *Kafnan* (clean, white unsewn sheets).

The body is then brought to a *Masjid* or public place where fellow Muslims, led by an *Imām,* pray over the deceased. If possible, the body is placed on its right side facing the *Qiblah*. The *Imām* stands behind the body and the followers form rows behind him, all facing the *Qiblah*.

Procedure for Ṣalāt al-Janāzah, According to the Mālikī School

1. Intention for the funeral prayer

2. First *Takbīr* (*Allāhu Akbar*), raising hands up to the ears
3. Praise of Allāh ﷻ, blessings on Rasūlullāh ﷺ and *du'ā'* for the dead person and for the remaining believers
4. Second *Takbīr* (*Allāhu Akbar*), raising hands as before
5. Repeat #3 above
6. Third *Takbīr;* repeat #3 above
7. Fourth *Takbīr;* repeat #3 above
8. *Salām* to the right side only

Procedure for Ṣalāt al-Janāzah, According to the Ḥanafī School

1. Intention for the funeral prayer.
2. First *Takbīr*, raising hands up to the ears and folding them together below the waist, not raising hands thereafter.
3. Second *Takbīr*, *Thana.*
4. Third *Takbīr*,*Ṣalawāt-'an-Nabī* (*Durūd Ibrāhīm*).
5. Fourth *Takbīr*, *du'ā'* for the dead person and for the remaining believers.
6. Fifth *Takbīr*.
7. *Salām* to the right side only.

Unlike any other prayer, *Ṣalāt-al-Janāzah* is offered standing up. The recitations during the *Ṣalāh* are done silently in Arabic.

There are several forms of recitation that can be used, such as:

وَالصَّلَوٰةُ وَالسَّلَامُ عَلَي مُحَمَّدٍ سَيِّدِ الْمُرْسَلِينَ اللّٰهُمَّ اغْفِرْ لِلْمُسْلِمِينَ

وَ ارْحَمْهُمْ وَاغْفِرْ لَنَا وَ ارْحَمْنَا بَعْدَهُمْ

Bismillāhi (a)r-Raḥmāni (a)r-Raḥīm. Wa (a)ṣ-Ṣalātu wa (a)s-salāmu `alā Muḥammadin sayyidi (a)-l-mursalīna. Allāhumma (a)ghfir lī (a)l-Muslimīna wa (a)r-ḥam-hum wa (a)ghfir lanā wa (a)rḥamnā ba`da-hum.

In the Name of Allāh, Most Gracious, Most Merciful.
All praise belongs to Allāh, Lord of the Universe. Peace and blessings of Allāh be with Muḥammad, leader of the Messengers (of Allāh). May Allāh forgive all the Muslims and have mercy on them; and may Allāh forgive us (too) and have mercy on us after them.

The longer and more popular version is:

اللَّهُمَّ اغفِرْ لِحَيِّنَا وَمَيِّتِنَا وَشَاهِدِنَا وَغَائِبِنَا وَ صَغِيرِنَا وَ كَبِيرِنَا
وَ ذَكَرِنَا وَ أُنْثَانَا
اللَّهُمَّ مَنْ اَحْيَيْتَهُ مِنَّا فَاَحْيِهِ عَلَي ألإسْلامِ
وَ مَنْ تَوَفَّيْتَهُ مِنَّا فَتَوَفَّهُ عَلَى الإيْمَانِ

Allāhumma (a)ghfir lī ḥayyinā wa mayyiti-nā wa shāhidinā wa ghā'ibina wa ṣaghīri-nā wa kabīri-nā wa dhakari-nā wa unthā-nā, Allāhumma man aḥyaita-hu min-nā fa aḥyihī `ala (a)l-Islām wa man tawaffaita-hu min-nā fa tawaffā-hū `ala (a)l-'Īmān.

O Allāh, forgive those of us who are still alive and those who have died, those who are present and those who are absent, the young amongst us and the old, the males and the females. O Allāh, the one from amongst us whom you wish to keep alive make him live according to Islām and the one whom you wish to die let him die in a state of Imān.

The body is then carried to the graveyard and buried in a simple grave, lying on its right side, facing the *Qiblah*.

Significance of Ṣalāt al-Janāzah

Ṣalāt-al-Janāzah (the Funeral Prayer) signifies our love, concern and respect for the dead, and sympathy for the bereaved family. We ask Allāh's Mercy for the deceased, by praising Allāh ﷻ and remembering Rasūlullāh ﷺ, whose *Shafā'ah* (intercession) we all seek. We are also reminded that our own death will come just as unexpectedly, so we must prepare for the Day of Judgement by making *Tawbah* (repentance) for our sins and trying to do good while in this world.

✔ EXERCISES

1. When is *Ṣalāt at-Tahajjud* normally offered?
2. When is *Ṣalāt at-Tarāwīḥ* offered?
3. What are the recommended number of *Raka`āt* for *Tarāwīḥ*?
4. How do we prepare a dead Muslim burial?
5. Describe how *Ṣalāt al-Janāzah* is offered.
6. How should the dead body be buried?
7. What is the significance of *Ṣalāt al-Janāzah*?

LESSON 28

ṢALAWĀT-AL-`ĪDAIN: `ĪD AL-FIṬR & `ĪD AL-'AḌḤĀ'

'Īd al-Fiṭr and *'Īd al-'Aḍḥā* are the two most important festivals for Muslims around the world. Before Rasūlullāh's ﷺ migration, it was the habit of the Madīnites to set aside two days each year for celebration and festivities. After Rasūlullāh ﷺ settled in Madīnah, he informed the Muslims that Allāh ﷻ had selected two better occasions for them to celebrate and thank Him: the days of *'Īd al-Fiṭr* and *'Īd al-'Aḍḥā*.

Preparation for 'Īd

Grooming

On the day of *'Īd*, Muslims should perform a ritual bath (*Ghusl*), dress in their best clothes, and put on perfume. It is reported by Ja'far ibn Muḥammad, who related from his father, on the authority of his grandfather that Rasūlullāh ﷺ used to wear his Yemani coat on the occasion of *'Īd*.

Traditional Meals on the Two 'Īds

It is the *Sunnah* of Rasūlullāh ﷺ to eat something before going out for the *Ṣalāh* on the day of *Īd al-Fiṭr*. It is reported by Anas ؓ that Rasūlullāh ﷺ did not go out on the day of *'Īd al-Fiṭr* until he had eaten an odd number of dates. On the day of *'Īd al-'Aḍḥā*, it was Rasūlullāh's habit to refrain from eating until he returned from the prayer.

How to Offer Ṣalāt al-'Īd

The *Ṣalawāt al-`Īdain* (the *Ṣalawāt* of the two *`Īds*) celebrate the two most important Islāmic festivals: *'Īd al-Fiṭr* and *'Īd-al-'Aḍḥā.* The same procedure is followed for the *Ṣalāwat* of both *`Īdain.*

The *`Īd* prayer is usually conducted in a large mosque or open space, so that all the people of the town or locality can gather to offer the *Ṣalāh* together. This special prayer may be offered from the time that the sun is three meters above the horizon until it reaches its meridian. Most of the scholars agree that it was the *Sunnah* of Rasūlullāh ﷺ to offer the *Ṣalāt al-'Aḍḥā* as early as possible to allow the people time to sacrifice their animals and to delay the *Ṣalāt al-Fiṭr* to give the people time to distribute the *Zakāt al-Fiṭr.*

Taking Different Routes To and From the Place of Prayer

Jābir ﷺ reported that on the day of *'Īd*, the Prophet ﷺ would go to the place of prayer from one route and return home following a different route. Thus, it is preferred to follow this *Sunnah.* However, there is no harm in following the same route to and from the place of prayer.

The *'Īd* prayer does not require *Adhān* or *Iqāmah,* since it is a *Nafl* prayer. The procedure is similar to that of the two-*Raka'āt Nawāfil Ṣalāh,* with the exception of some additional *Takbīrāt*, as follows:

1. After making the intention for *'Īd Ṣalāh,* the *Imām* and followers begin the *Ṣalāh* with *Takbirāt-al-Iḥrām.*
2. The *Imām* calls six additional *Takbīrāt*, which the congregation follows, each time raising their hands to their ears, as in the first *Takbīr*. The rest of the first *Rak'ah* follows the same procedure as the first *Rak`ah* of any *Farḍ Ṣalāh.*
3. The second *Rak`ah* begins with six *Takbīrāt.* The rest of the second *Rak'ah* follows the same procedure as the second *Rak`ah* of the two-*Raka'āt Farḍ Ṣalāh.*
4. The *Ṣalāh* is followed by a special *Khuṭbah* delivered by the *Imām.* It is an important part of the *'Īd* prayer and must be

listened to attentively.

Rasūlullāh ﷺ urged all Muslims; men, women, and children; to attend the *'Īd Ṣalāh*.

The Day of 'Īd al-Fiṭr

'Īd al-Fiṭr is a special Islāmic festival of thanksgiving and celebration marking the end of Ramaḍān. It occurs on the first day of Shawwāl.

Breaking the fast on the morning of *'Id al-Fiṭr* with dates or any other sweet is *Sunnah*, and marks the beginning of the celebration . The *'Īd* celebration is a dignified Islāmic affair, characterized by meeting, exchanging greetings and gifts, and remembering our less fortunate brothers and sisters through charity.

Zakāt-al-Fiṭr is distributed to the needy before entering the Masjid, preferably on the previous evening, to allow the recipients to prepare for the festival (see Lesson 37).

The Days of 'Īd al-Aḍḥā

This festival takes place on the tenth day of the month of Dhul-Ḥijjah and it commemorates Prophet Ibrāhīm's willingness to sacrifice his beloved son, Ismā'īl ﷺ, in obedience to the commandment of Allāh ﷻ. Because Allāh ﷻ was merely testing Ibrāhīm's faith, He sent a ram to be sacrificed in Ismā'īl's place. This is why the sacrifice of camels, goats, cow, rams, and other animals marks the celebration of *'Īd al-'Aḍḥā*

'Īd al- 'Aḍḥā also corresponds with one of the most important days of *Ḥajj*. As you will learn in Lesson 43, the *Ḥujjāj* offer the same sacrifice on this day in Mina.

Like all other Islāmic forms of worship, *'Īd al-'Aḍḥā* is characterized by thanking Allāh ﷻ, sharing with other believers, and enjoying the festival in an Islāmic spirit. The distribution of the sacrificial meat is an example of this spirit. It is divided into three parts: one-third is distributed to the poor and needy, one-third to friends and relatives, and the remaining one-third is kept for the home. Especially during the days of *`Īd,* no Muslim, however needy and poor, should go hungry or helpless.

✔ EXERCISES

1. What are the two great Islāmic festivals?
2. Is there an *A<u>dh</u>ān* or *'Iqāmah* for *Ṣalāt al-`Īd*?
3. During what time may *Ṣalāt al-`Īd* be offered?
4. What is the difference between *Ṣalāt al-'Īd* and any other two-*Rak`āt* *Ṣalāh*, such as *Fajr Ṣalāh*?
5. When is *'Īd al-Fiṭr* held and what does it commemorate?
6. When is *'Īd al-'Aḍḥā*, and what does it commemorate?
7. How is the sacrificial meat for the festival of *'Īd al-'Aḍḥā* distributed?
8. Describe the spirit of *'Īd al-'Aḍḥā.*

LESSON 29

SPECIAL PRAYERS

Ṣalāh for Rain

Previously, we discussed how Allāh ﷿ is the ultimate controller of the universe, including all the things we refer to as natural phenomena. One such phenomenon is the rain.

Rain provides water, essential for the survival of all living things. Without it, crops could not grow, there would be no food for animals and human beings, and the climate would become unbearably hot and dry. Truly, Allāh ﷿ sends the rains as a sign of His mercy.

No one can control rainfall, and even with all the advanced technology available today, predicting rainfall is often very difficult. Thus, when rain is much delayed, it is recommended that Muslims pray to Allāh ﷿ as follows.

In the morning, after sunrise but before noon, the worshipers should assemble to offer the *Ṣalāh* in an open space or mosque. Following a two-*Rak'ah Ṣalāh*, in which *al-Fātiḥah* and another *Sūrah* are recited aloud, a sermon may be given. Then, the worshipers should stand and raise their hands and eyes towards the heavens and pray to Allāh ﷿ for rain. The *du`ā'* may be as follows:

اَللّٰهُمَّ اسْقِ عِبَادَكَ وَ بَهِيْمَتِكَ وَ انْشُرْ رَحْمَتَكَ وَ أَحْيِ بَلَدَكَ الْمَيِّتَ

O our Lord! Send Your rain to Your servants and Your animals.
Shower Your mercy on us, and revive Your dead land!

Ṣalāh During an Eclipse of the Sun

A solar eclipse takes place when the moon passes between the sun and the earth, blocking the sun's light from the earth. In accordance with Allāh's universal laws, such eclipses occur at regular intervals, which scientists can now calculate and predict with accuracy.

By chance, there happened to be an eclipse of the sun when Rasūlullāh's young son, Ibrāhīm ﷺ, died. Inadvertently, some of his people assumed that this phenomenon occurred as a result of the tragedy. However, Rasūlullāh ﷺ rejected this as superstition, clarifying:

> *The eclipse of the sun or the moon is only a sign of the greatness of Allāh ﷻ, and does not take place for death or life of anybody. Whenever you see such an eclipse, hasten to pray to Allāh ﷻ.*
>
> (Transmitted by Bukhārī)

Thus, prayer during an eclipse is an important *Sunnah* for every Muslim who has reached the age of maturity. The *Ṣalāh* consists of two *Raka`āt* in which the Qur'ānic selections are to be read out loud. In each *Rak'ah, al-Fātiḥah* and the *Rukū'* (bowing) are offered twice.

Ṣalāh at the Eclipse of the Moon

A lunar eclipse takes place when the earth passes between the sun and the moon, casting the earth's shadow on the moon. The *Ṣalāh* during an eclipse of the moon consists of two *Raka`āt* offered in the same way as the *Ṣalāh* during a solar eclipse. However, it is recommended to pray it individually at home.

✔ EXERCISES

1. Describe how to offer the *Ṣalāh* for rain.
2. What causes an eclipse of the sun?
3. Describe how to offer the *Ṣalāh* during an eclipse of the sun.
4. What causes an eclipse of the moon?
5. Describe how to offer the *Ṣalāh* during an eclipse of the moon.
6. What is the significance of the *Ṣalāh* during an eclipse of the sun or moon?

LESSON 30

INTRODUCTION TO AṢ-ṢIYĀM

Definition of Ṣawm

Aṣ-Ṣiyām literally means abstinence. Fasting in Islām means to avoid eating and drinking and abstinence from all forms of sexual pleasure between dawn and sunset.

The fast should be preceded by a formal intention of *Ṣawm*, specifying whether it is a *Farḍ* fast (such as the Ramaḍān fast), a *Nafl* fast (voluntary fast) or a fast for any other reason.

The Purpose and Spirit of Ṣawm

The purpose of *Ṣawm* is to seek *Taqwā* (heightened spiritual awareness of Allāh ﷻ). In denying oneself food, drink, and other basic needs, one becomes deeply aware of Allāh's power. With this awareness comes the desire to submit completely to His power and earn His mercy.

To truly benefit from the experience of fasting, a Muslim should purify his thoughts and actions to gain the pleasure of Allāh ﷻ. One should focus his energies in the remembrance of Allāh ﷻ by spending extra time in prayer, being charitable and forgiving towards others, and avoiding un-Islāmic behavior.

Types of Ṣawm

One of two types of *Ṣawm* may be offered: *Farḍ* (obligatory) or *Nafl* (voluntary).

Examples of *Farḍ Ṣawm*:

A. The Ramaḍān fast

During the lunar month of Ramaḍān, *Ṣawm* is *Farḍ* for every adult Muslim. Under certain circumstances, one may be excused from *Ṣawm* or be allowed to postpone it.
(This will be explained in Lesson 32.)

B. *Kaffārah*: Fast of Expiation

It is *Farḍ* for a person who has deliberately nullified his fast or failed to fast in the month of Ramaḍān to make atonement through *Kaffārah*. (The details will be presented in Lesson 34)

C. *Nadhr*: Fast of Vowing

If someone vows to fast, the fast becomes *Farḍ* for him.

II. Examples of *Nafl Ṣawm*:

A. It is recommended to fast voluntarily at any time of the year, except on days when fasting is prohibited.

B. In accordance with the *Sunnah* of Rasūlullāh ﷺ, it is recommended to fast voluntarily on Mondays and Thursdays. It is also recommended to fast on the 1st, 11th and 21st day of each Islāmic month.

III. Days when *Ṣawm* is prohibited:

A. *Ṣawm* is prohibited on *'Īd* days and the two days following *`Īd al-Aḍḥā*.

✔ EXERCISES

1. Define *Ṣawm* in Islām.
2. What is the purpose of *Ṣawm*?
3. How should a Muslim behave while he is in the state of *Ṣawm*?

4. Name three kinds of *Farḍ* fasts.
5. Which days are recommended for voluntary *Ṣawm?*
6. On which days is it prohibited to fast?

LESSON 31

THE FAST OF RAMAḌĀN

When to Begin the Fast of Ramaḍān

The fast is to begin the day following the appearance of the new moon for the month of Ramaḍān. If it is confirmed that the moon has been sighted in any part of the world, a Muslim should begin his fast on dawn the following day.

Intention to Fast

The Muslim must make his formal intention of *Ṣawm* before dawn. He may make the intention for the whole month of Ramaḍān, or he may make the intention to fast one day at a time. However, if he chooses the latter, he must remember to renew his intention every night for the next day's fast.

When making the intention to fast for the whole month of Ramaḍān, a person may declare in his mind:

نَوَيتُ صَومَ شَهرِ رَمضانَ الحَاضِرِ فَرْضاً لِلّهِ تَعالى

I intend to fast for the month of Ramaḍān, as a Farḍ act of worship to You. I pray You to accept the fast from me.

If a person's fast is interrupted for some days due to illness, menstruation, travel, or other reasons, he or she must renew the intention before resuming the fast.

The Suḥūr: Pre-dawn Meal

It is recommended for a Muslim to take *Suḥūr*, a pre-dawn meal. To eat this meal is the *Sunnah* of Rasūlullāh ﷺ and it is intended to reduce the hardship of *Ṣawm* during the day.

However, if due to over-sleeping or any other cause, a person finds that it is already dawn, or if he is not certain whether dawn has come, he should refrain from eating or drinking. It is safest to awake early enough to eat and finish the meal about 20 minutes before dawn, since eating after dawn would nullify the day's fast.

The Ifṭār

As soon as the sun has set, the Muslim should break his fast with *Ifṭār* (breakfast). If the *Ifṭar* is light; for example, a few dates or other fruit and water; one may have it before offering the *Maghrib* (Sunset) *Ṣalāh.* However, if one is having a heavy *Ifṭār*, one should offer the *Maghrib Ṣalāh* first to avoid missing its proper time.

✔ EXERCISES

1. When should a Muslim start fasting the *Farḍ* fast of Ramaḍān?
2. When and how is the intention made for *Ṣawm?*
3. What is *Suḥūr,* and when is it eaten?
4. What is *Ifṭār,* and when is it eaten?

LESSON 32

EXEMPTION FROM ṢAWM DURING RAMAḌĀN

Those Who Should Fast

During the month of Ramaḍān, *Ṣawm* is *Farḍ* for every Muslim who has reached physical maturity. For girls, this is normally marked by the start of menstruation, and for boys, by the first emission of semen.

Those Who Should Not Fast

Those who should not fast include: (a) women during menstruation; (b) women during the blood of childbirth. However, after the month of Ramaḍān, they should fast an equal number of days to those missed.

Those Who Have a Valid Excuse to Postpone Ṣawm

If necessary, the following types of people are allowed to defer *Ṣawm*:

(a) ***The sick:*** if the *Ṣawm* is likely to make the illness worse.
(b) ***The mentally ill:*** for as long as the mental illness lasts.
(c) ***The traveler:*** if his journey is more than 77 kilometers and serves a purpose permissible by the *Sharī'ah* (i.e., not stealing, drinking, gambling, etc.) If the traveler began his journey after dawn, it is not permissible to suspend the day's fast. However, if the traveler leaves after dawn with the intention of *Ṣawm* and is overcome by exhaustion due to *Ṣawm* later in the day, he may suspend the day's fast.
(d) ***The pregnant woman:*** if the *Ṣawm* is likely to harm the

health of the mother or her unborn child.

(e) ***The nursing mother:*** if the *Ṣawm* is likely to harm the health of the mother and/or prevent her from having enough milk for her baby.

After the end of Ramaḍān, these people should fast an equal number of days to those missed.

Those Who Are Excused From Ṣawm

The following types of people are completely exempt from *Ṣawm* and are not required to make up days missed:

(a) ***The chronically ill:*** those who suffer from a serious, permanent illness that would be made worse by fasting.

(b) ***The permanently mentally ill***

(c) ***The very old:*** those who are too old and weak to fast at any time of the year.

Instead, it is recommended that the permanently ill or old person should do *'Iṭ`ām* (i.e. distribute alms in the form of staple foodstuff: rice, dates, etc.) at the rate of one *Muddan Nabī* for each day of the Ramaḍān fast. (A *Muddan Nabī* is what can be contained by two hands of average size cupped together.)

✔ EXERCISES

1. At what age does it become *Farḍ* for a Muslim to fast in Ramaḍān?
2. Name two conditions that may prevent a woman from fasting. Do such women have to fast the number of days missed after Ramaḍān?
3. Name five types of people who are allowed to postpone the *Ṣawm* in Ramaḍān.
4. Under what three conditions is a traveler allowed to break his fast.

5. Name three types of people who are excused from the fast of Ramaḍān altogether.
6. What should a very old person who cannot fast do instead?

LESSON 33

CONDITIONS THAT NULLIFY ṢAWM; QAḌĀ'

The Qaḍā' for Ṣawm

Qaḍā' means restitution for a missed fast. If a person does not fast, or if his fast is nullified for any of the reasons listed below, he should make up the fast after Ramaḍān. The conditions that necessitate *Qaḍā'* are:

(a) ***Illness:*** When recovered, a person should fast the number of days equal to the number missed after Ramaḍān.

(b) ***Travel*:** After Ramaḍān, a person should fast a number of days equal to the number of days missed in travel.

(c) ***Intravenous feeding, injections for nutritional purposes, etc:*** This includes any type of feeding by means other than eating and drinking. However, other medical injections, such as vaccinations, do not nullify the fast.

(d) ***Forgetfulness:*** If a person eats, drinks, smokes, or engages in sexual activity, forgetting that he is fasting, he does not need to do *Qaḍā'*. However, if he remembers that he is fasting and continues to eat, drink, etc., on purpose, he will have to do both *Qaḍā'* and *Kaffārah.*

There are a number of other things that nullify a fast and require *Qaḍā'*, but the above are considered the most important ones to remember at this stage.

When to Do Qaḍā'

A Muslim who has to do *Qaḍā'* may do it any time after the month of

Ramaḍān, but it is advisable not to delay it without cause. No one knows how soon life may end, and one may not have time to make restitution. If a Muslim carelessly delays his *Qaḍā'* until after the Ramaḍān of the following year, he should do both *Qaḍā'* and *'Iṭ'ām,* i.e. giving out alms of *Muddan Nabī* (one handful) of staple foodstuff for each day of *Qaḍā'*.

✔ EXERCISES

1. What is the meaning of *Qaḍā'* ?
2. If a Muslim unintentionally eats something during the Ramaḍān fast, what should he do?
3. Name three things that make it necessary to do *Qaḍā'*.
4. If someone is given a shot (injection), is his fast rendered void?
5. What is *'Iṭ'ām*?

LESSON 34

CONDITIONS THAT NULLIFY ṢAWM: KAFFĀRAH

The Seriousness of Nullifying a Fast

The conditions that necessitate *Qaḍā'* (mentioned in the last lesson) fall into two categories:

1. Unforeseen circumstances, such as illness or traveling, which make the fast physically difficult or impossible.
2. Accidental circumstances, such as unintentional forgetfulness.

However, if an adult Muslim refuses to fast in Ramaḍān without a valid excuse, or breaks his fast intentionally without a valid excuse, his case is much more serious. The Ramaḍān fast is *Farḍ*, a pillar of Islām, and any Muslim who refuses to observe the fast shows direct disobedience to Allāh ﷻ and commits a sin. If he repents and wishes to clear himself of that sin, he must do both *Qaḍā'* and *Kaffārah* for each day he broke his fast. In all cases, *Kaffārah* is preceded by *Qaḍā'*.

Kaffārah: Expiation

There are three ways of doing the *Kaffārah*; only one needs to be executed. They are listed below in order of preference:

1. Give alms of staple foodstuff to 60 needy Muslims at the rate of one *Muddan Nabi* (one handful) per person. If two days of fasting have been rendered void, one should give out food in the same manner and quantity for two days. If 30 days of Ramaḍān fast have been rendered void, he should give out food in the same manner and quantity for 30 days.

2. Free a female slave (if such a situation is applicable) for each nullified fast.
3. Fast continuously for two lunar months (i.e. about 60 days) for each day that his fast was rendered void.

Conditions That Necessitate Kaffārah

1. The *Kaffārah* is necessary only for the breaking of a Ramaḍān fast. It is not necessary for the breaking of any other fast.
2. The breaking of the fast must be intentional, not due to forgetfulness or compulsion by another person.

There are other rules for the *Kaffārah*, but the above ones are considered the most important at this stage.

✔ EXERCISES

1. Why is it a serious offense for an adult Muslim to intentionally nullify a Ramaḍān fast or to refuse to fast without a excuse?
2. If an adult Muslim's fast is intentionally nullified during Ramaḍān, or if he refused to fast without excuse and then wished to expiate his sin, what should he do?
3. What are the three ways of doing *Kaffārah*?
4. If a Muslim starts a day of voluntary fast and decides to eat at midday, his fast becomes void. Should he do *Kaffārah*?
5. (a) In the month of Ramaḍān, if a Muslim forgets that he was fasting and eats something by mistake, should he do *Qaḍā'* only, or *Qaḍā'* and *Kaffārah?*
   (b) If a Muslim broke his Ramaḍān fast by accident, realized his mistake, and then deliberately went on to eat more food, should he do *Qaḍā'* only, or *Qaḍā'* and *Kaffārah*?

LESSON 35

EXTRA WORSHIP DURING RAMAḌĀN

How to Increase the Benefits of Ṣawm

The benefits of fasting are increased if a Muslim uses the month of Ramaḍān to improve his other acts of worship. Through extra efforts towards purifying one's thoughts, increasing acts of charity, offering extra *Ṣalāh,* and paying special attention to the reading and understanding the Qur'ān, one can develop a deeper spiritual awareness and closeness to Allāh ﷻ.

Ṣalāt at-Tarāwīḥ

It is highly recommended to offer additional *Sunnah Raka`āt* of *Ṣalāt-at-Tarāwīḥ* with *Jamā`ah* after the *'Ishā'* prayer. *Ṣalāt at-Tarāwīḥ* may be offered individually, but it is preferable to offer it in *Jamā`ah,* either at the *Masjid* or with the family at home.

The number of *Raka`āt* of *Ṣalāh* in *Tarāwiḥ* varies between 10 and 20. Generally, three *Raka`āt* of *Ṣalāt al-Witr* are offered in *Jamā`ah* after *Tarāwiḥ..*

The *Ṣalāt at-Tarāwīḥ* is offered in sets of two *Raka'āt* each. The worshipers should make the intention of *Ṣalāt at-Tarāwīḥ* at the beginning of the *Ṣalāh* for all the *Raka'āt* they intend to offer or at the beginning of each pair of *Raka`āt*. If they are offering the *Ṣalāh* behind an *Imām,* they should also make the intention to follow him. Each pair of *Raka`āt* includes the recitation of *al-Fātiḥah* and a *Sūrah* out loud, in the same way as in *Ṣalāt al-Fajr.*

Traditionally, the *Imām* of the *Tarāwiḥ* prayer is both a *Ḥāfiẓ* (one who has memorized the whole Qur'ān) and a *Muqrī* (one who knows the art of reciting the Qur'ān with *Tajwīd*). Starting at the beginning *(Sūrat-al-Fātiḥah)*, each day, the *Imām* recites a portion of the Qur'ān, completing the reading over the last ten days of the Ramaḍān. However, completion of the Qur'ān is not a condition of the *Tarāwiḥ*.

Lailat al-Qadr: The Night of Power

This is the night in which the Qur'ān was revealed to Rasūlullāh ﷺ. The Qur'ān informs us:

شَهْرُ رَمَضَانَ ٱلَّذِىٓ أُنزِلَ فِيهِ ٱلْقُرْءَانُ هُدًى لِّلنَّاسِ
وَبَيِّنَٰتٍ مِّنَ ٱلْهُدَىٰ وَٱلْفُرْقَانِ

Ramadān is a month in which was sent down the Qur'ān, as a guide to humankind, also clear (Signs) for guidance and judgement (between right and wrong).
(*Al-Baqarah* 2:185)

On *Lailat-al-Qadr,* the Night of Power, Rasūlullāh ﷺ received his first *Waḥī* (revelation of the Qur'ān) as he sat in the cave of Hira. According to the Qur'ān:

إِنَّآ أَنزَلْنَٰهُ فِى لَيْلَةِ ٱلْقَدْرِ ﴿١﴾ وَمَآ أَدْرَىٰكَ مَا لَيْلَةُ ٱلْقَدْرِ ﴿٢﴾
لَيْلَةُ ٱلْقَدْرِ خَيْرٌ مِّنْ أَلْفِ شَهْرٍ ﴿٣﴾ تَنَزَّلُ ٱلْمَلَٰٓئِكَةُ وَٱلرُّوحُ
فِيهَا بِإِذْنِ رَبِّهِم مِّن كُلِّ أَمْرٍ ﴿٤﴾ سَلَٰمٌ هِىَ حَتَّىٰ مَطْلَعِ ٱلْفَجْرِ ﴿٥﴾

Indeed, We have revealed this (Qur'ān) in the Night of Power. And what will explain to you what the Night of Power is? The Night of Power is better than a thousand months. Therein, come down the angels and the Spirit descend therein, by the permission of their Lord with all

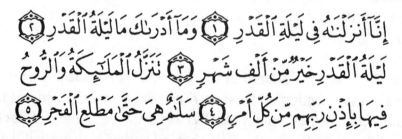

decrees.(That night is) Peace, until the rising of the dawn.
(*Al-Qadr*: 97-1-5)

Every righteous Muslim makes a special effort to find this night and make the best out of it. Rasūlullāh ﷺ is reported to have said:

Look for Lailat al-Qadr in the last ten nights of Ramaḍān.
(Transmitted by Bukhārī)

There are other *Aḥādīth* which indicate that this night occurs in the last ten odd nights of Ramaḍān. One particular *ḥādīth* especially draws attention to the night of the 27th. Not knowing the exact night is also a blessing. Every believer puts forth an extra effort to find the Night of Power in the last 10 nights through sincere prayer and worship. He or she not only benefits from the Night of Power, but is rewarded many times over for the extra sincere worship in the blessed month of Ramaḍān.

I'itikāf

I'itikāf refers to a religious retreat in the *Masjid* for the sole purpose of engaging in worship, without distraction or interruption, in an effort to draw closer to Allāh ﷻ.

A person may engage in *I'itikāf* any time of the year. The period of seclusion may be between 10 and 30 consecutive days. According to the tradition of Rasūlullāh ﷺ, it is best to include the last ten days of Ramaḍān.

The man (or woman) in *I'itikāf* spends his/her time in *Ṣalāh*, asking Allāh's forgiveness *(Istaghfār)*, remembrance of Allāh ﷻ *(Dhikr)*, reading the Qur'ān and invoking Allāh's blessings on the Prophet *(Ṣalāt `ala an-Nabī)*.

A person should begin *I'itikāf* with intention. He or she should then stay in the *masjid,* day and night, and should not leave it except to go to the bathroom, buy essential provisions nearby, or take a bath.

✔ EXERCISES

1. Name three ways in which a Muslim can increase the benefits of *Ṣawm.*
2. When is *Ṣalāt at-Tarāwīḥ* offered?
3. How many *Raka`āt* are usually offered in *Tarāwīḥ?*
4. What does the Qur'ān say about the *Lailat al-Qadr?*
5. When is *Lailat al-Qadr* expected to be?
6. What is the meaning of *I'itikāf*?
7. Which acts of worship should a person do while in *I'itikāf*?
8. On what days did Rasūlullāh ﷺ make *I'itikāf*?

LESSON 36

THE BENEFITS OF ṢAWM

Spiritual and Moral Benefits

Ṣawm is an act of obedience to Allāh ﷻ. There are countless spiritual and moral benefits to it. A fasting person is willing to sacrifice his basic worldly needs in submission to Allāh's Will, seeking His pleasure and blessings. In his hunger and thirst, he can feel the essence of Allāh's immense power.

Ṣawm trains a Muslim in *Taqwā* (awareness of Allāh ﷻ). During the fast, this awareness holds him back from eating and drinking, despite temptation. *Ṣawm* also tests his sincerity, because only Allāh ﷻ can know if a person is sincerely fasting, or if he secretly breaks his fast.

Ṣawm teaches good behavior and discipline. *Ṣawm* does not only abstinence from eating and drinking. A fasting Muslim must also try to control all his improper behavior. Rasūlullāh ﷺ is reported to have said:

If one does not abandon falsehood in words and deeds,
Allāh ﷻ has no need of his abandoning his food and drink.
(Transmitted by Bukhārī)

By being patient in hunger, we learn to exercise self-control in all difficulties. A Muslim learns to be the master of his desires rather than a slave of his desires.

Ṣawm helps us appreciate the Bounties of Allāh ﷻ. A thirsty person is truly grateful when he finds water, while one who can drink water all day may take water for granted.

Social Benefits

Ṣawm unites Muslims all over the world. It unites rich and poor, male and female, educated and uneducated. Whatever their status, they share the same experience of sacrifice to please Allāh ﷻ.

Ṣawm helps us empathize with those who suffer poverty and hardship. By feeling the effects of hunger and thirst, a Muslim can better understand the suffering of the others. He/she is more inclined to give charity to the needy.

The bonds of Islāmic brotherhood are renewed by social visits and gatherings during Ramaḍān. Muslims are encouraged to invite others to join them in *Ifṭār,* prayer, and recitation of the Qur'ān at this time.

Health Benefits

Scientific research shows that fasting is healthy for the body. By giving certain organs a break from the normal processes of digestion, circulation, and excretion, the blood becomes purified, and certain stomach ailments improve. It also helps people to break the unhealthy habits of smoking and overeating.

Thus, fasting not only offers rewards in the Hereafter, but offers numerous benefits in this world as well.

✔ EXERCISES

1. Name as many of the spiritual and moral benefits of *Ṣawm* as you can remember.
2. Name three social benefits of *Ṣawm.*
3. How does *Ṣawm* benefit our health?

LESSON 37

INTRODUCTION TO ZAKĀH

What is Zakāh?

Zakāh literally means "to purify." It is the fourth pillar of Islām and therefore it is *Farḍ* (obligatory) on every Muslim male and female. *Zakāh* is a type of welfare tax that we pay our poor Muslim brothers and sisters. Through *Zakāh*, we become aware of our obligations to our fellow human beings.

Zakāh is mentioned many times in the Qur'ān:

خُذْ مِنْ أَمْوَٰلِهِمْ صَدَقَةً تُطَهِّرُهُمْ وَتُزَكِّيهِم بِهَا

Take alms of their wealth so that you may cleanse them, thereby, and cause them to grow in purity.
(*At-Tawbah* 9:103)

Paying *Zakāh* cleanses and purifies us by replacing selfishness and greed with satisfaction gained by sharing our good fortune with those less fortunate. At the same time, *Zakāh* helps those in need out of their difficulties. By making each Muslim responsible for the welfare of the brothers and sisters in his or her community, *Zakāh* fosters feelings of equality and brotherly love among all members of society.

Who Pays Zakāh?

A Muslim, whether male or female, must pay *Zakāh* when his/her wealth has reached a certain determined amount called the *Niṣāb*. If his/her wealth is below the value of *Niṣāb*, he/she pays nothing. In the case of gold, silver or currency (including bank savings), *Niṣāb* should have been in the person's possession for a period of one year.

Niṣāb

Niṣāb refers to the minimum amount of wealth and property on which *Zakāh* should be paid. According to the *Sharī'ah*, a person who possesses property exceeding the *Niṣāb* for at least a year is capable of paying *Zakāh*. The *Sharī'ah* has determined a fixed a *Niṣāb* for different assets, such as currency, gold, silver, minerals, crops, property, animals, etc. Calculation of the *Niṣāb* on various items is a complicated science which you may learn later. In Lesson 38, we have briefly discussed the *Niṣāb* of some items.

Who Should Receive Zakāh?

According to the Qur'ān, there are eight categories of people who are given permission to receive *Zakāh* (*Sūrah At-Tawbah* 9:60). They are as follows:

1. The Poor: This includes those who do not have enough food for one year's sustenance.

2. The Needy: This includes the destitute, i.e. those who are not sure of having food for one day.

3. Collectors of the Funds: If the Muslim state or the Muslim community employs people to collect the *Zakāh*, they are entitled to part of it (if they are in need of it).

4. Those Whose Hearts are to be Reconciled: These include new converts to Islām, particularly those who may have suffered financial or other loss because of rejection or persecution by their people.

5. Freeing Prisoners-of-War or Slaves: This refers to those captured in war. They may be bought or ransomed using *Zakāh* money, and then freed. This is one of the many Islāmic measures against slavery.

6. The Indebted: This includes those people who are weighed down with debts which they have no means by which to clear their debts.

7. In the Way of Allāh ﷻ: This covers all uses of money for the defense and propagation of Islām. Islāmic organizations dedicated to spreading the message of Islām in our own age are eligible to receive *Zakāh*.

8. The Wayfarer: This refers to a person who is stranded on a journey and in need of financial help.

The Zakāh and the Ṣadaqah

In the Qur'ān, the term *Ṣadaqah* is sometimes used to include *Zakāh* and all forms of charity. However, *Zakāh* is a *Farḍ*, a required duty. The time of giving and the amount to be given are fixed. On the other hand, *Ṣadaqah* is a general term meaning 'charity.' It can be any amount given at any time to any person. This charity may be in the form of money, food or clothing.

Rasūlullāh ﷺ mentioned that an act of kindness could also be *Ṣadaqah* (charity). Thus, removing harmful objects from the road, helping someone to load his vehicle, or even smiling at someone is a form of *Ṣadaqah*. Therefore, every person, whether rich or poor, has the means to give *Ṣadaqah*, help his/her relatives and neighbors, and win Allāh's pleasure.

✔ EXERCISES

1. What is the *Zakāh?*
2. What is the benefit of *Zakāh:*

(a) to the one who gives it?
(b) to the one who receives it?
(c) to the society as a whole?

3. What is meant by *Nisāb?*
4. What are the eight classes of people that are entitled to *Zakāh*?
5. What is the meaning of giving *Zakāh* "in the way of Allāh سبحانه وتعالى"?
6. What is the difference between *Zakāh* and *Ṣadaqah?*
7. Name some ways in which a student or a poor person can give *Ṣadaqah.*

LESSON 38

DETERMINING THE ZAKĀH ON VARIOUS ITEMS

Zakāh on Gold, Silver and Currency

The *Niṣāb* for gold, silver and currency depends on the current value of gold, which changes from time to time. In traditional Arab currency, the *Niṣāb* for gold is 20 *Dinārs* (gold coins), the *Niṣāb* for silver is 20 *Dirhams* (silver coins), and the *Niṣāb* for currency is the value of 200 *Dirhams.*

The amount to be given as *Zakāh* is two and a half percent, or one-fortieth, of any savings of one year or more.

The currency of a country in the form of coin or paper is subject to *Zakāh* based upon its purchasing power. The currency is actually backed by silver and gold, therefore the amount of currency owed equals the amount of *Niṣāb* for silver (200 Dirhams or 14½ ounces).

Zakāh on Items of Trade

Similarly, *Zakāh* is also paid on the value of items for trade; such as cloth, books, machinery, cars, etc. Items for trade and business should be in the person's possession for a period of one year. The *Niṣāb* for these goods is calculated as two and a half percent of the cash value.

Zakāh on Livestock

Zakāh must be paid once a year on livestock; such as cows, camels, sheep and goats; when their number has reached the level of the *Niṣāb*. The following lists the *Niṣāb* for ownership of livestock and the *Zakāh* owed accordingly.

Number of cows owned	*Zakāh* to be given
30 to 39	1 two-year-old cow
40 to 59	1 three-year-old cow

Number of sheep or goats owned	*Zakāh* to be given
40 to 120	1 one-year-old sheep or goat
101 to 200	2 sheep or goats
201 to 399	3 sheep or goats
400 and above	1 sheep or goat for each hundred owned

Zakāh on Grains an Crops

Allāh ﷻ says in the holy Qur'ān:

يَٰٓأَيُّهَا ٱلَّذِينَ
ءَامَنُوٓا۟ أَنفِقُوا۟ مِن طَيِّبَٰتِ مَا كَسَبْتُمْ وَمِمَّآ أَخْرَجْنَا
لَكُم مِّنَ ٱلْأَرْضِ ۖ

O Believers! Spend of the good things which you earned, and of that which We bring forth from the earth for you
(*Al-Baqarah* 2: 267)

Zakāh is to be paid on crops whenever a crop is harvested. It is to be paid on wheat, rice and other grains, all kinds of beans and peas, groundnut, dates, olives, and their equivalents in various parts of the world. As recommended by Rasūlullāh ﷺ, the *Niṣāb* for farm produce if the land is irrigated naturally (by a spring, rainfall, or a river) is one-tenth, and if it is irrigated by drawing water from a well or dam, the *Niṣāb* is one half of one-tenth.

Zakāh is not required on fruits and vegetables which perish quickly when picked, such as oranges, bananas, pineapples, mangoes, guavas, lettuce spinach, tomatoes, peppers, etc.

The *Niṣāb* for grains and crops is 1,200 *Muddan Nabī* by volume. (A *Muddan Nabī* is what can be contained by two hands of average size held together.)

✔ EXERCISES

1. What is the percentage of *Zakāh* on currency? (Choose one of the following)
   (a) 10
   (b) 2½
   (c) 5
   (d) 7½
2. What is the percentage of *Zakāh* on items of trade such as cars, cloth, books etc.? (Choose one of the following)
   (a) 12%
   (b) 5
   (c) 2½
   (d) 10
3. Which of the following items should *Zakāh* be paid on? (Choose as many as are applicable)
   (a) A woman's personal gold jewelry
   (b) A rice-crop
   (c) A student's books
   (d) A book-sellers books
   (e) A herd of 40 cows
   (f) A bank deposit
4. How often should *Zakāh* be paid on livestock?
5. If a man has 130 sheep, what would be the *Zakāh* on them?
6. When should *Zakāh* be paid on grains and crops?
7. Name five types of grain or crops on which *Zakāh* should be paid.
8. Name five fruits or vegetables on which *Zakāh* is not paid.
9. The *Zakāh* on grains and crops which are not irrigated artificially is (choose one):

(a) one-fifth (b) one-tenth (c) one-twentieth

10. What is a *Muddan Nabī*?

11. What is the *Zakāh* on grains and crops?

12. *Zakāh* must be paid on savings in your possession over a certain period of time. What is this time period?

LESSON 39

ZAKĀT AL-FIṬR

What is Zakāt al-Fiṭr?

Zakāt al-Fiṭr is a compulsory charity due at the end of Ramaḍān. Every Muslim; young and old, male and female, who has more than enough food to last him and his family 24 hours, is responsible for *Zakāt al-Fiṭr*. If a person has dependents, he must pay *Zakāt-al-Fiṭr* for each of them (e.g. wife, children and other dependent relatives).

Calculating the Amount of Zakāt al-Fiṭr

The amount of *Zakāt al-Fiṭr* due on behalf of each person, adult or child, is one *sa'*, which is equal to approximately three kilograms of grain, such as barley, corn, rice, wheat, etc. We can also pay the equivalent cash value instead.

When and to Whom is Zakāt al-Fiṭr to be Given?

Zakāt al-Fiṭr is to be given to the poor on the 29th or 30th of Ramaḍān, when the new moon of Shawwāl is sighted. It may even be given on the day of *'Īd* before the *'Īd Ṣalāh*, but it is advised not to delay it until after the *Ṣalāh*.

The Benefits of Zakāt al-Fiṭr

Sometimes, despite our most earnest efforts, we may unintentionally engage in inappropriate behavior that might have reduced the rewards of our fast.

The payment of *Zakāt al-Fiṭr* serves as atonement for such behavior and purifies our fast.

Making Muslims responsible for each other provides all of us, rich or poor, the opportunity to celebrate *'Īd al-Fiṭr,* a joyous occasion which marks the end of the Ramaḍān fast.

✔ EXERCISES

1. Who should give *Zakāt al-Fiṭr*?
2. What amount per person should be given as *Zakāt al-Fiṭr*?
3. When should *Zakāt al-Fiṭr* be given?
4. What are the benefits of *Zakāt al-Fiṭr*?

LESSON 40

INTRODUCTION TO ḤAJJ AND `UMRAH: THE PILGRIMAGE

What is Ḥajj?

Ḥajj, the fifth pillar of Islām, is the pilgrimage to the Ka`bah in Makkah on specific dates in the month of *Dhu al-Ḥijjah.* It is also the largest gathering of worshipers of any faith in the world. Allāh ﷻ says in the Qur'ān:

وَلِلَّهِ عَلَى ٱلنَّاسِ حِجُّ ٱلْبَيْتِ مَنِ ٱسْتَطَاعَ إِلَيْهِ سَبِيلًا ۚ

Pilgrimage to the Sacred House is a duty to Allāh for humankind, for him who is able to make the journey.
(*Āl-'Imrān* 3: 97)

We will discuss some major aspects of *Ḥajj* here, and our readers can study it in greater details in the special books which are written for the *Ḥujjāj* (pilgrims) when, *insha' Allāh*, they have the honor of performing *Ḥajj.*

The pilgrimage season starts in the month of *Shawwal* while the actual pilgrimage is performed from 8th to 13th of *Dhu al-Ḥijjah.* If a pilgrim visits the Ka`bah at any other time of the year, he cannot perform *Ḥajj,* but he can perform *`Umrah,* which will be discussed in Lesson 45. *An `Umrah* in *Ḥajj* season is a part of the *Ḥajj.* The *Ḥajj* requires the completion of certain procedures which we shall refer to as the rites of *Ḥajj*.

Those for Whom Ḥajj is Farḍ

As a pillar of Islām, *Ḥajj* is a *Farḍ* duty for every mentally capable, adult

Pilgrims performing *Tawāf* of the Ka'bah during *Ḥajj*.

Muslim (male or female). One should perform *Ḥajj* at least once in his or her lifetime, provided he or she has enough money for the journey, is healthy enough to undertake the journey, and the journey does not involve particular danger (e.g. traveling through a war-zone).

There is no harm in children accompanying their parents for *Ḥajj*. However, it does not exempt them from having to complete *Ḥajj* when they become mature adults.

There are three ways of performing pilgrimage. The pilgrim should make his intention according to the one he chooses to perform. The types of pilgrimage are:

1. *Ifrād* (*Ḥajj* Only): The pilgrim performs only the *Ḥajj*.
2. *Qiran* (Combined *Ḥajj*): The pilgrim performs the *Ḥajj* and *'Umrah* (the Lesser Pilgrimage) together, without a break with one Ihrām.
3. *Tamattu`* (*Ḥajj* with Ease): The pilgrim performs the *'Umrah* during the *Ḥajj* season with one *Ihrām* and then opens *Ihrām*. He performs *Ḥajj* with other *Ihrām in* the same season.

The Rites of Ḥajj in Sequence

We shall only deal with *Ḥajj Tamattu`* in this book, which is generally performed by the *Ḥujjāj* who come from abroad. *Ḥajj Tamattu'* is performed in two installments with two separate *Ihrāms*. In the first part, the *Ḥajj* performs the *'Umrah*, and in the second part, he performs *Ḥajj*. The procedure for the *'Umrah* is the same whether it is done as part of the *Ḥajj* or independent of the *Ḥajj*.

The Performance of `Umrah

The first part of the *Ḥajj Tamattu'*, as we mentioned earlier is the performance of the rites of *`Umrah* which are descrbed here briefly:

1. *Iḥrām*: formal intention and entrance into the state of consecration by putting on *Iḥrām*
2. *Talbiyah*: announcement of one's arrival for the sole purpose of performing *Ḥajj*
3. *Ṭawāf:* going round the Ka`bah on arrival to Makkah seven times.
4. *Du`a* at the *Multazim*
5. Drinking from the water of Zamzam
6. *Sa'ī:* the walk between the hills of Ṣafā and Marwah

The above steps would complete the rites of *`Umrah*. The people who are performing only *`Umrah* or *Ḥajj Tamattu`* would now make *Halq* (shaving of hairs of the head) or *Taqsīr* (cutting the hair) and open the *Iḥrām*. The *Ḥujjāj* making *Ḥajj Tamattu`* would wait for 8 th of *Dhu al-Ḥijjah* to put on *Iḥrām* of *Ḥajj* again.

Performance of Hajj

1. Spending the night of 8 th *Dhu al-Ḥijjah* at Mina
2. Standing at 'Arafāt on the 9 th of *Dhu al-Ḥijjah*
3. Spending the night of 9 th *Dhu al-Ḥijjah* at Muzdalifah
4. Stoning the *Jamrāt-al-'Aqaba* in Mina on the 10 th of *Dhu al-Ḥijjah*;
5. Offering sacrifice of an animal in Mina on the 10 th of *Dhu al-Ḥijjah* (if applicable)
6. Making *Halq* (shaving) or *Taqsīr* (cutting the hair) and opening the *Iḥrām*.
7. *Ṭawāf-ul-Ifāḍa* (*Ṭawāf* of the Crowd): i.e. going around the Ka`bah seven times. This *Ṭawāf* is followed by the *Farḍ Sa'ī* of *Ḥajj*, to be done according to the type of *Ḥajj* the pilgrim has intended.
8. Stoning the three *Jamrāt* daily in Mina, for two or three days, depending on the circumstances.

9. The Farewell *Ṭawāf:* circumambulating the Ka`bah for the last time.

The *Ḥajj* rites are now complete and most of the *Ḥujjaj* leave to visit *Masjid an-Nabi* in Madinah and offer *Ṣalāh* and *Salām* on Rasūlullāh ﷺ. The *Ḥujjāj* who arrive early in Makkah often visit Madinah first and get ready to leave for their homes after *Ḥajj*. The visit to Madinah is a journey of love and is not the part of the *Ḥajj* ritual.

The Farḍ Rites of Ḥajj

The *Farḍ* rites of *Ḥajj* are:

a. Formal intention and entrance into the state of *Iḥrām* (the state of consecration)
b. *Ṭawāf* (circumambulating the Ka`bah)
c. *Sa'ī* (the walk between Ṣafā and Marwah)
d. *Wuqūf* (standing at Arafāt)

If any of these four rites is omitted, the *Ḥajj* is invalid.

✔ EXERCISES

1. What is *Ḥajj* and in what season it is performed?
2. What conditions make the *Ḥajj Farḍ*?
3. Describe the three ways of performing *Ḥajj*
4. What are the four *Farḍ* rites of *Ḥajj*?
5. What is the difference between *Ḥajj* and *`Umrah* rites?

LESSON 41

PREPARATION FOR ḤAJJ: ENTERING IḤRĀM

The Mīqāt

In this chapter, we shall discuss the rites of *Ḥajj* in greater detail. On the way to Makkah, pilgrims coming from various directions enter the state of *Iḥrām* at certain assembly points, called *Mīqāt* in Arabic.

Pilgrims, arriving by air from any part of the world, pass their *Mīqāt* before landing in Jeddah. If they intend to go directly from Jeddah to Makkah, they should either enter *Iḥrām* before boarding the plane, or before they pass the *Mīqāt*. Sometimes, airlines make such anouncements to help the *Ḥujjāj*. In case they are not able to put on *Iḥrām*, they must do so in Jeddah, but they must sacrifice a sheep as *hadyā* (atonement for having passed the *Mīqāt* before entering *Iḥrām*.) However, if these pilgrims had the intention to go to Madinah first, they must do so. No *Iḥrām* is required for a visit to Madinah. After the visit to Madinah as they go to Makkah for the *`Umrah*, they would enter *Iḥrām* at a place called *Dhu (a)l-Ḥulaifāh* . No *hadyā* would be necessary in that case.

Requirements of Iḥrām

1. Entering *Iḥrām* at the prescribed *Mīqāt*;
2. Bathing to cleanse the whole body before entering *Iḥrām*. It is also recommended to trim the nails and hair;
3. For men, putting on two pieces of unsewn white cloth, leaving the head bare; sandals should not cover the heels. Female dress should cover everything but the face and hands;
4. *Wuḍū'* followed by a two-*Rak'ah Ṣalāh*;
5. Formal intention for *Ḥajj*, including the type of *Ḥajj* one intends: *Ifrāḍ*, *Qiran* or *Tamattū`*;

6. *Talbiyah*: announcing one's arrival for *Ḥajj*, from the time of entering *Iḥrām* until arrival to Arafāt. The pilgrims call out together:

Labbaika Allāhumma Labbaik	*Here I am, O Allāh! Here I am!*
Labbaika lā -sharīka la-ka Labbaik	*Here I am (bearing witness that) You have no partner! Here I am!*
Inna (a)lḥamda wa a(n) ni'mata la-ka	*Certainly, all praise and grace belongs to You*
Wa (a)l-mulka la-ka lā sharīka la-ka	*And Kingship belongs to you, You have no parners.*

Acts Prohibited While in the State of Iḥrām

The following must be avoided once the *Iḥrām* is entered:

a. Hunting or killing a living thing;
b. Sexual pleasure of any kind;
c. Shaving or cutting the hair;
d. Trimming the nails;
e. Wearing perfume, cologne, or cosmetics.

The Significance of Iḥrām

All the acts and prohibitions of the state of *Iḥrām* help bring the pilgrim to a higher state of mind. Removing himself from worldly affairs and his everyday life, he puts on the same simple dress as every other pilgrim, and he becomes undistinguished. The words of the *Talbiyah* and the wearing of the *Iḥrām* bring him to a state of submission to Allāh ﷻ, and prepare him for the rites of pilgrimage.

✔ EXERCISES

1. What is a *Mīqāt*?
2. If a pilgrim from the United States plans to fly directly to Jeddah and continue directly from Jeddah to Makkah, when should he enter *Iḥrām*?
3. What is *Talbiyah*?
4. What does a man wear when he enters *Iḥrām*?
5. What does a woman wear when she enters *Iḥrām*?
6. Name three things that are forbidden while in *Iḥrām*.

LESSON 42

PERFORMING THE 'UMRAH

Ṭawāf: Circling the Ka'bah

A Pilgrim must enter the *Haram* in *Iḥrām* with *Wuḍu'*. Next, he should stand near the Black Stone and make intention for *Ṭawāf*. With the declaration: *Allāhu Akbar!* (Allāh ﷻ is Most Great), he begins circumambulating the Ka'bah seven times in an anti-clockwise direction, with the Ka'bah to his left.

At the beginning of each round, the pilgrim should try to kiss the Black Stone, declaring: *'Allāhu Akbar.* If this is not possible, one should try to touch it with the hand, declaring: *'Allāhu Akbar,'* and place his hand on his mouth (without kissing it). If this is also not possible, one should point towards the stone and say: *'Allāhu 'Akbar.'*

While circling the Ka'bah, the pilgrim should make personal *du'ā'* (supplication) for himself, his parents and others, simultaneously glorifying Allāh ﷻ.

As soon as the seven rounds are completed, it is Sunnah that the pilgrim should make *du'a* at the *Multazim* and then offer two *Raka'āt* of *Wajib at-Ṭawāf Ṣalāh*, preferably at a place called *Maqām Ibrāhīm* (the Station of Ibrāhīm ﷺ). If that area is too crowded, one may pray anywhere in the mosque.

It is also a *Sunnah* to drink the water of Zamzam standing, facing Ka'bah in three breaths as much as one could drink. Rasūlullāh ﷺ advised us that when drinking Zamzam make special *Du'a* for whatever intention this water is drunk Allāh ﷻ grants that *Du'a*. This marks the end of the *Ṭawāf*. Without delay, the pilgrim should proceed to perform *Sa'ī*.

Sa'ī: Walking Between Ṣafā and Marwah

Sa'ī is made between two low hills, Ṣafā and Marwah, located a short distance from the Ka`bah. The pilgrim starts at Ṣafā. Facing the Ka`bah, he makes the intention for *Sa'ī*. After declaring, *'Allāhu Akbar'*, he hastens to Marwah. Pilgrims are required to run a short distance along the way. This rite reminds us of the story of Hajrah ﷺ, who ran in search of water for her infant son, Ismā`il. Her love and concern for her son pleased Allāh ﷻ, and He rewarded her for her faith with the spring of Zamzam.

The pilgrim makes seven trips between Ṣafā and Marwah, finishing his *Sa'ī* at Marwah. Whenever one mounts the hills of Ṣafā or Marwah, *'Allāhu Akbar'* should be declared. Throughout the process of *Sa'ī*, one should glorify Allāh ﷻ and make personal *du'a* . At the end of the seventh round *Ḥajj* must pray to Allāh ﷻ and make *Ḥalq* or *Taqsīr* of his head. Women clip one lock of their hair, which is about one inch.

The *`Umrah* is now complete. Those who come to perform *`Umrah* are now free to return. The *Ḥujjāj* who are performing this *`Umrah* in *Ḥajj* season as part of *Ḥajj Tamattu'* must wait for the 8th of *Dhu al-Hijjah* , at which time, they shall put on *Iḥrām* of *Ḥajj* and go to Mina for the remaining rites.

✔ EXERCISES

1. What is *Ṭawāf*?
2. How many times does a pilgrim circle the Ka`bah in *Ṭawāf*?
3. In which direction does a pilgrim circle the Ka`bah: clockwise or anti-clockwise?
4. After circling the Ka`bah, the pilgrim offers two *Raka`āt* of *Nafl Ṣalāh*. Where should he try to offer this *Ṣalāh*?
5. What is *Sa'ī*?
6. What does *Sa'ī* commemorate?

7. What are Ṣafā and Marwah?
8. How many times does a pilgrim walk between Ṣafā and Marwah?
9. On which hill does the pilgrim begin his *Sa`ī*?
10. What is Arafāt? (a) a plain; (b) a mountain; (c) a lake
11. What is done in *Wuqūf*?

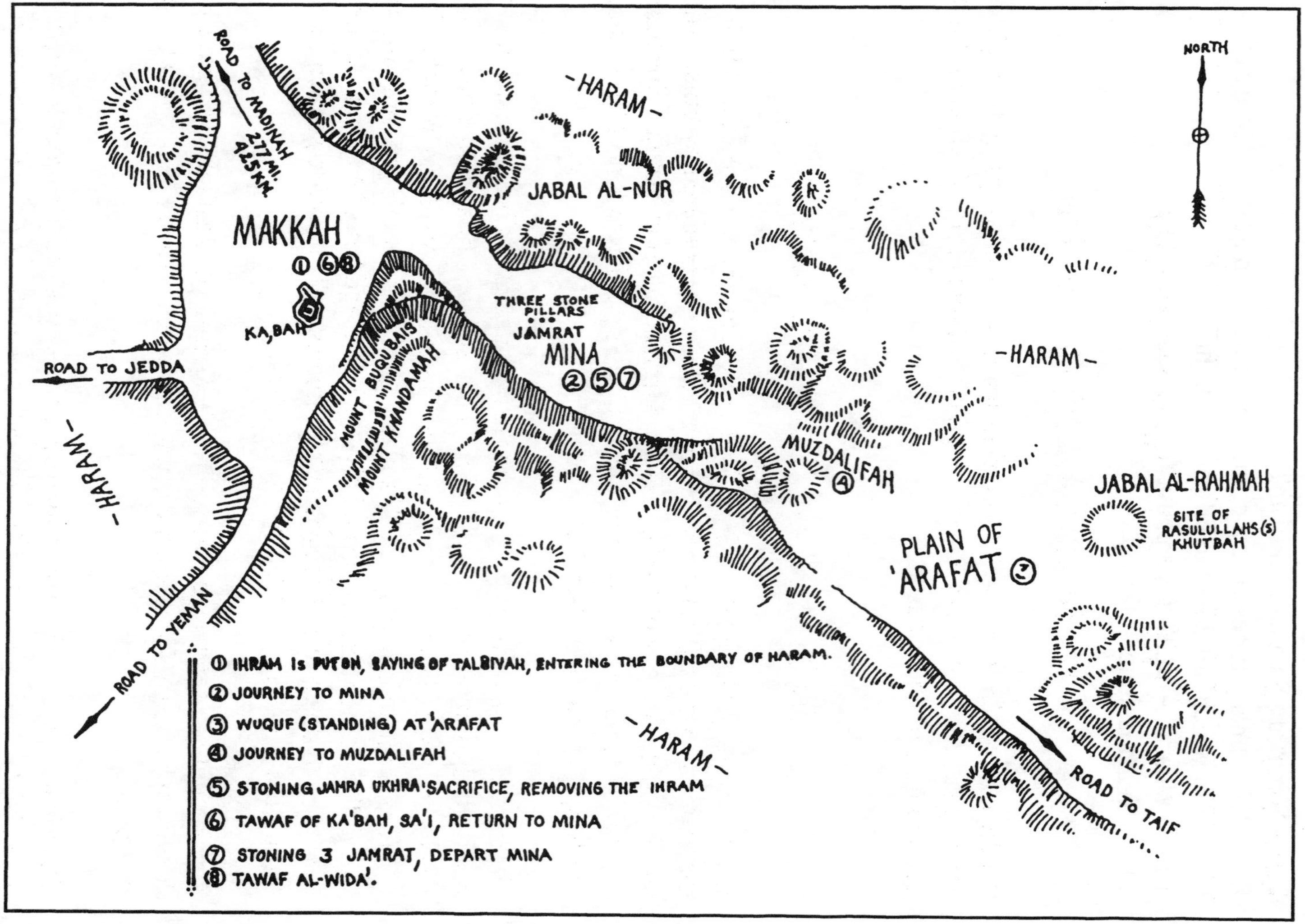
NORTH
-HARAM-
ROAD TO MADINAH 277 MI. 425 KM.
JABAL AL-NUR
MAKKAH
① ⑥ ⑧
KA'BAH
ROAD TO JEDDA
THREE STONE PILLARS
JAMRAT
MINA
② ⑤ ⑦
MOUNT BUQUBAIS
MOUNT KHANDAMAH
-HARAM-
-HARAM-
MUZDALIFAH ④
JABAL AL-RAHMAH
SITE OF RASULULLAHS(S) KHUTBAH
PLAIN OF 'ARAFAT ③
ROAD TO YEMAN
ROAD TO TAIF
-HARAM-
① IHRAM IS PUT ON, SAYING OF TALBIYAH, ENTERING THE BOUNDARY OF HARAM.
② JOURNEY TO MINA
③ WUQUF (STANDING) AT 'ARAFAT
④ JOURNEY TO MUZDALIFAH
⑤ STONING JAMRA UKHRA' SACRIFICE, REMOVING THE IHRAM
⑥ TAWAF OF KA'BAH, SA'I, RETURN TO MINA
⑦ STONING 3 JAMRAT, DEPART MINA
⑧ TAWAF AL-WIDA'.

The plan of the Ḥajj

LESSON 43

THE CHRONOLOGY OF ḤAJJ

The 8th of Dhu al-Ḥijjah: To Mina

On the 8th of *Dhu al-Hijjah*, all pilgrims leave Makkah to spend the night at Mina, a suburb of Makkah, continuing their *Talbiyah* (glorification of Allāh ﷻ) and quiet meditation.

The 9th of Dhu al-Hijjah: Wuqūf at Arafāt

On the morning of the 9th of *Dhu al-Hijjah*, the pilgrims move from Mina to the plain of 'Arafāt. It is beyond Mina, a wide plain, bordered by hills. After sunrise on the 9th day of *Dhu al-Ḥijjah*, pilgrims gather at `Arafāt. Spending the day at Arafāt is the most important rite of *Ḥajj*. There is no *Ḥajj* without the *Wuqūf* (standing at 'Arafāt).

Upon entering 'Arafāt, the pilgrims make the intention of being present at this divinely chosen place as part of *Ḥajj*. They stay at Arafāt until sunset. The *Ẓuhr* and *'Aṣr* prayers are combined and shortened to two *Raka'āt* each. The pilgrims remain standing until sunset, glorifying Allāh ﷻ, praying for Rasūlullāh ﷺ, for himself, his relatives, friends, and other Muslims. If tired, they may sit down to rest occasionally. Females are allowed to remain seated during the entire stay at 'Arafāt , if they wish.

The Mount of Mercy (Jabal ar-Rahmah), wherefrom Rasūlullāh ﷺ gave his famous historical *Ḥajj* sermon calleed *Khutbah al-Wadā',* is also located on this plain.

The *Ḥujjāj* must leave 'Arafāt soon after sunset without performing *Maghrib*. The *Ṣalāh* of *Maghrib* must be combined with the *'Isha* and performed at

The 10th of Dhu al-Ḥijjah: Night at Muzdalifah

Muzdalifah is located halfway between 'Arafāt and Mina. The *Ḥujjāj* spend the night in this open field. As soon as they arrive, they must offer the combined *Ṣalāh* of *Maghrib* and *`Ishā'*, preferably in the *Masjid Mash`ar al-Ḥarām.* They must spend the night in prayer, rest and collecting pebbles to do Rami *Jimar*, stone the *Jamrāt*, the three symbolic *Shaiṭāns* when they return to Mina. After the *Fajr Ṣalāh*, the pilgrims move to the sacred monument, *Mash`ar al-Ḥarām.* The *Ḥujjāj* must offer the *Ṣalāt al-Fajr* with *Jamā`ah* and do *Wuqūf* (Praying in the standing position) until daybreak. Then, they return to Mina, where they throw seven small stones at *Jamrāt al-`Uqba*, the largest of the *Jamrāt*. The *Jamrāt* are three stone pillars symbolizing the *Shaiṭān*. By stoning them, we resolve never to follow the *Shaiṭān* in the path of evil and wrong-doing.

After throwing the stones, the pilgrims offer a sacrifice of a sheep, goat, cow, or camel in Mina. However, pilgrims performing the single *Ḥajj* (*Ifrād*) need not offer animal sacrifice, unless there is a special reason for it. Since the 10th of *Dhu al-Ḥijjah* is the day of *'Īd al-'Aḍḥā*, Muslims all over the world offer animal sacrifice also. Following the sacrifice, pilgrims shave their heads or have a haircut. They come out of *Iḥrām* and change into regular clothes.

Next, the pilgrims leave for Makkah to perform the *Farḍ Ṭawāf* of *Ḥajj*, or *Ṭawāf al-Ifāḍah*. This *Ṭawāf* is best done on the day of sacrifice, but may be done later on, if necessary. If doing *Ḥajj Tamattu`* (*Ḥajj* for pleasure), one should perform *Sa'ī* after the *Ṭawāf*.

11th and 12th of Dhu (a)l-Ḥijjah: The Days of Tashrīq

It is obligatory to pass the night of 10th and 11th *Dhu al-Ḥijjah* in Mina. The following two days are spent in Mina in prayer. Every pilgrim is required to do *Rami Jimār* (stoning seven times each *Jamrah*) for all the three *Jamarāt*,. If a pilgrim decides to stay the night of 12th he must perform *Rami Jimār* after mid-day (*Zawal*) on the third day before he leaves the Mina.

Ṭawāf al-Widā: The Farewell Ṭawāf

It is *Sunnah* to pay a last visit to the Ka`bah for a farewell *Ṭawāf* just before departure from Makkah.

✔ EXERCISES

1. Where do pilgrims go on the 8th of *Dhu al-Ḥijjah*?
2. Where do pilgrims go on the 9th of *Dhu al-Ḥijjah*?
3. Name four things pilgrims do on the 10th of *Dhu al-Ḥijjah*.
4. What are the *Jamarāt*?
5. What is the significance of throwing stones at the *Jamarāt*?
6. Which festival do all Muslims celebrate on the 10th of *Dhu al-Ḥijjah*?
7. What is *Ṭawāf al-Ifāḍah*?

LESSON 44

THE ḤAJJ CODE OF CONDUCT

Conditions That Invalidate the Ḥajj

If even one of the *Farḍ* rites of *Ḥajj* is omitted or improperly performed, the *Ḥajj* is considered invalid. As stated in previous lessons, these include: *Iḥrām* (entering into a state of consecration); *Wuqūf* (standing at Arafāt); *Tawāf al-Ifāḍah* (the *Farḍ Ṭawāf* of *Ḥajj*); *Sa'ī* (walking between Ṣafā and Marwah). In addition, any sexual activity will also invalidate *Ḥajj*. This not only includes sexual intercourse, but also emission of semen due to contact with the opposite sex or prolonged sexual thoughts.

Necessity of Completing and Repeating an Invalidated *Ḥajj*

Even if a pilgrim is aware that his *Ḥajj* has been nullified, he should complete the other rites of *Ḥajj*. The *Ḥajj* should then be repeated the following year, or as one is able to do so.

Menstruation During Ḥajj

Menstruation does not invalidate or ruin the *Iḥrām* or *Ḥajj*. However, *Ṭawāf* should be avoided during menstruation. If a woman is menstruating, she should delay her *Ṭawāf* and *Sa'ī* (as required) until her period is over. She should then perform *Ghusl* and then complete her *Ṭawāf*. This can be done at any time during the rest of the month of *Dhu al-Ḥijjah*.

The Ḥajj Code of Conduct

The atmosphere during *Ḥajj* is unlike any other a Muslim can experience. First of all, the pilgrim finally is given the opportunity to see the birthplace of Islām and our beloved Rasūlullāh ﷺ. Being in the presence of the Ka`bah gives the feeling of being very close to Allāh ﷻ. Sharing this experience with thousands of other Muslims gives an overwhelming sense of the universal strength of Islām. Truly, the *Ḥajj* is the ultimate sacred journey.

Out of respect for its sanctity, the *Ḥajj* should devote complete attention to the correct performance of *Ḥajj* to avoid any discrepancies. In addition, he should maintain good behavior and relations with other pilgrims. The Qur'ān says:

ٱلْحَجُّ أَشْهُرٌ مَّعْلُومَٰتٌ ۚ فَمَن فَرَضَ فِيهِنَّ ٱلْحَجَّ فَلَا رَفَثَ
وَلَا فُسُوقَ وَلَا جِدَالَ فِى ٱلْحَجِّ ۗ وَمَا تَفْعَلُوا۟ مِنْ خَيْرٍ
يَعْلَمْهُ ٱللَّهُ

And whoever undertakes the pilgrimage in those (months) shall on pilgrimage, abstain from lewd speech, from all wicked conduct, and from quarreling; and whatever good you do, Allāh is aware of it.
(*Al-Baqarah* 2:197)

Thus, for a successful *Ḥajj*, a pilgrim must learn self-control and set a high standard of behavior for himself. He should also try to maintain it in his daily life after his return from *Ḥajj*.

✔ EXERCISES

1. What conditions invalidate *Ḥajj*?
2. If a pilgrim's *Ḥajj* becomes invalid, what should he do?
3. If a woman is menstruating, does this affect her *Ḥajj*?

4. What kind of behavior does the Qur'ān warn the pilgrims against during *Ḥajj*?
5. Visit a *Ḥajj* in your community and interview him on his experiences.

LESSON 45

THE VISIT TO MADĪNAH

One of the greatest desires of a Muslim is to visit Madinah, pray at the *Masjid an-Nabi*, offer *Salām* to Rasūlullāh ﷺ standing at his grave, and visit the many blessed places that relate to the life of Rasūlullāh and his *Ṣahābah* رضي الله عنهم. The visit to Madinah is not a part of the *Ḥajj* rites, yet every *Ḥajj* feels his mission incomplete without a visit to this "Illuminated City" (*Madinah al-Munawwarah*). Like Makkah, Madinah is also considered *Ḥaram*, as it is the second holiest city of Islam. The journey from Makkah to Madinah is filled with lots of emotions, as the *Ḥujjāj* make their way to Madinah saying *Salām* and with the praises of Rasūlullāh ﷺ in their hearts and on their lips.

Ṣalāh in the Rawḍah

Upon arrival to Rasūlullāh's mosque in Madīnah, the pilgrim should offer two *Raka'āt* of *Tahiyyat al-Masjid Ṣalāh,* preferably in the area of the mosque called the *Riyāḍ al-Jannah*. Rasūlullāh ﷺ said:

The area between the minbar and my house is one
of the gardens of Paradise (Riyad al-Jannah).
(Transmitted by Bukhāri)

The area of *Riyāḍ al-Jannah* is often overcrowded. In such circumstances, one may offer it anywhere else in the mosque. After completing this *Ṣalāh*, the pilgrim must make a special *Du'a*.

Ṣalāh for Rasūlullāh ﷺ and his Ṣaḥābah

The *Ḥajj* should then move to *Mawajah Sharīf*, the area facing the grave of

Rasūlullāh ﷺ. He should stand there respectfully and recite *Salām* and *Ṣalāt `ala an-Nabi.* The first two *Khulafa'*, Abū Bakr رضي الله عنه and 'Umar رضي الله عنه are also buried next to Rasūlullāh ﷺ. The pilgrim should pray for Allāh's Mercy and Blessings on Abū Bakr رضي الله عنه and 'Umar رضي الله عنه, respectively. Then, he should turn toward the *Qiblah* and pray to Allāh ﷻ for humanity, the *`Ummah*, family, friends and himself.

One should not pray to Rasūlullāh ﷺ or make *Sajdah* toward his grave. Sometimes, certain people, out of love for Rasūlullāh ﷺ, commit certain acts which are *Shirk*, without realizing their evil. Rasūlullāh ﷺ warned us against all such acts. True love of Rasūlullāh ﷺ is to follow his *Sunnah*.

Concluding Ṣalāh in the Riyāḍ al-Jannah

After this, the *Ḥajj* should return to the *Rawḍah,* or any other part of the *Masjid* available, and recite further *Ṣalāh* for Rasūlullāh ﷺ and his family. This is a good time for the pilgrim to ask Allāh's forgiveness for his own sins. He should invoke Allāh's Blessings and Mercy for his parents, relatives and all Muslims and ask for the guidance of humanity to the path of Islam.

Another important spot in the *Masjid* is the *Suffah*, an elevated platform on the north side of the *Masjid.* It was the residence of *Aṣḥab as-Ṣuffah* (People of the Platform), Rasūlullāh's رضي الله عنهم *Ṣaḥābah* who had no homes and lived there. The *Ṣuffah* was the first residential university of Islam.

Visit to Jannat al-Baqī`

Jannat al-Baqī`* is the graveyard of Madinah. Thousands of *Ṣahābah, at-Tabi`un and many pious ancesters of the *`Ummah* are buried here. The grave of `Uthmān رضي الله عنه, the third of the *Rashidūn khalifah, Ummahat al-Mu'minīn* (except Khadijah رضي الله عنها, who is buried in *Jannat al-Ma`lā* in Makkah), the four daughters of Rasūlullāh ﷺ and many other members of his family and

Masjid-an-Nabawi, Madinah Munawwarah

his *Ṣahābah* are located here. A *Ḥajj* generally visits the *Baqī`* and offers *Du`a* for these blessed souls.

Other Attractions in Madīnah

There are many important places and Mosques to visit in Madinah which include:

1. ***The Battlefield of Uḥud***: Under the Mountain of Uḥud, where the battle of Uḥud was fought in the 3 AH. Amīr Hamzah' ﷺ, the uncle of Rasūlullāh ﷺ, and other *Shuhada'* are buried here. Rasūlullāh ﷺ loved this mountain of Uḥud.
2. ***The Sab`ah Masajid***: In the field where the battle of Aḥzab or Ditch was fought stand seven small mosques. These mosques represent the tents of Rasūlullāh ﷺ and other important *Ṣahābah.*
3. ***Masjid Qiblatain*** (The Mosque of the Two *Qiblahs*): This *Masjid* stands at the spot where the *Ṣahābah* were offering the *Ṣalāt al-Aṣr* when someone announced to them the command of Allāh ﷻ to change the *Qiblah* (Direction) from *Bait al-Maqdas* to *Bait Allāh.* During the *Ṣalāh,* they turned to *Bait Allāh* and completed the *Ṣalāh.*
4. ***Masjid Qubā'***: This was the first *Masjid* established in Madinah by Rasūlullāh ﷺ as he entered the city. If one makes *Wuḍu'* and goes to the *Masjid* with the intention of offering two *Rak`at* of *Nawafil*, he gets the reward of one *`Umrah.*
5. ***Masjid Jum`ah***: Rasūlullāh ﷺ offered his first Jum`ah of Madinah in this place. It was in the neighborhood of Banu Salem..
6. ***Masjid Ghamamah***: Rasūlullāh ﷺ offered the *Ṣalāh* for *`Idain* (*Id al-Fiṭr* and *`Id al-'Aḍḥa*) and other special prayers in this *Masjid.*

The Purpose of Visiting Madīnah

Madīnah is the location of Masjid an-Nabi, and we go there to offer *Ṣalāh* and *Salām* to him and visit the mosques and historical places associated with the life of Rasūlullāh ﷺ and his *Ṣaḥābah* ؓ. By seeing the Masājid, grave and other historical sites, the pilgrim is reminded of the sacrifices made by the early Muslims, and this enhances the *Ḥajj* experience and strengthens his faith and conviction. One must return from Madinah and *Ḥajj* with the commitment to follow the teachings of the Qur'ān and the *Sunnah* and avoid what is forbidden.

✔ EXERCISES

1. What should a pilgrim do at the mosque in Madīnah when he goes to visit Rasūlullāh ﷺ?
2. Name the two companions of Rasūlullāh ﷺ who are buried close to his grave?
3. Which other places in Madīnah may a pilgrim choose to visit?
4. What is the importance of *Masjid al-Quba* and *Masjid al-Qiblatain*?
5. Should we pray to Rasūlullāh ﷺ and make *Sajdah* to his grave?
6. How can we express our true love for Rasūlullāh ﷺ?
7. Is the visit to Madinah part of the *Ḥajj*? What is the real purpose of the visit?

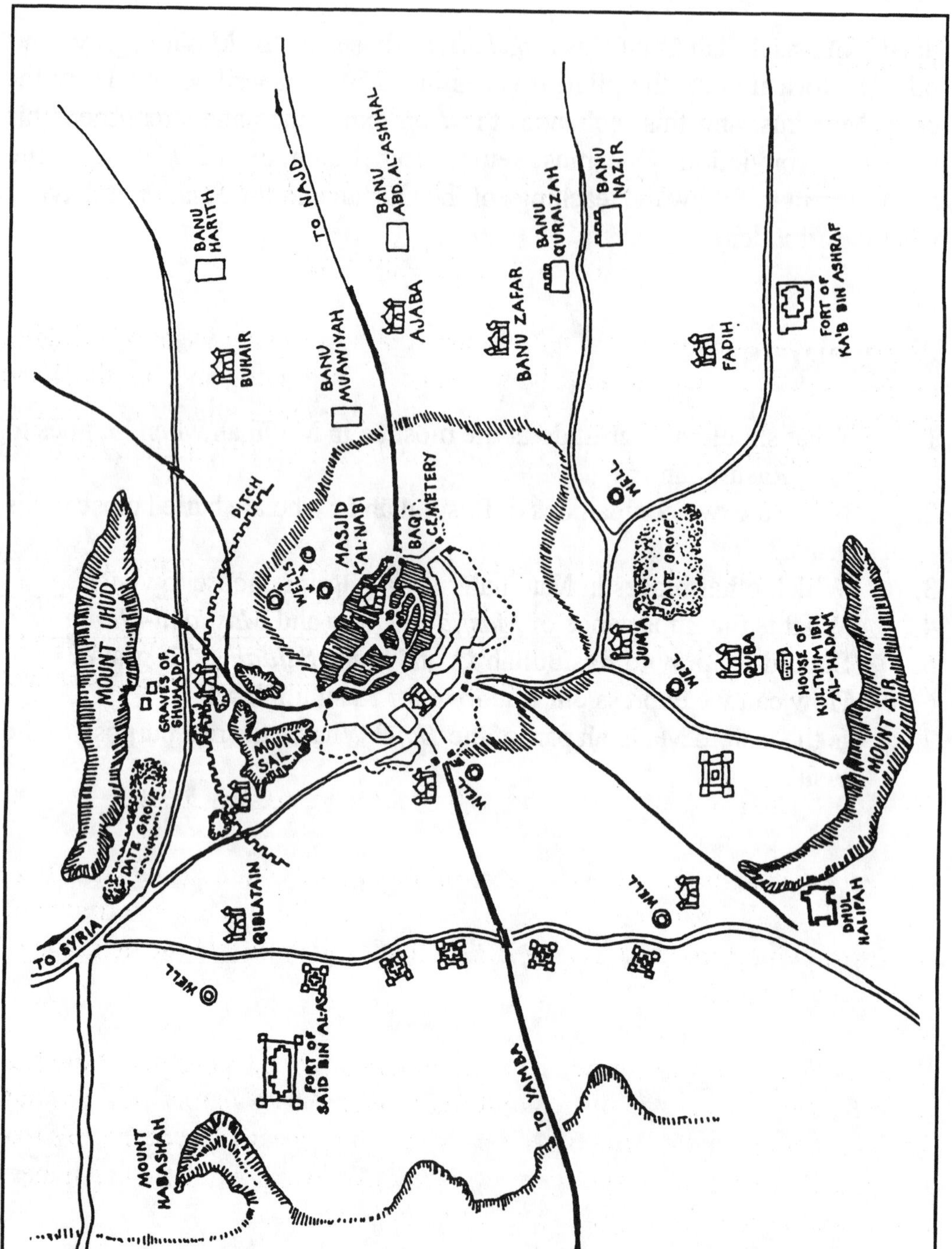

The map of Madinah

LESSON 46

THE SIGNIFICANCE AND BENEFITS OF ḤAJJ

The Greatest Gathering

As we have discussed in earlier lessons, Islām has many ways of bringing people together. On a daily basis, Muslims come together in the local mosque, and on Fridays, at the *Jam'a Masjid*, a larger mosque. On *'Īd* days, they assemble in even larger numbers for the *'Īd* prayer. By far, the *Ḥajj* is the greatest gathering of all.

Every year, *Ḥajj* brings Muslims from all parts of the world together in a great act of worship. Pilgrims from every nation meet in peace for the *Ḥajj*. They participate in the greatest demonstration of Islāmic brotherhood, which serves to unify the Muslim *'Ummah* against all forms of racial and ethnic prejudice.

Spiritual Enrichment and Strengthening of Faith

The *Ḥajj* commemorates the sacrifices of Prophets Ibrāhīm ﵇ and Ismā'īl ﵇, who built the Ka`bah and prayed there. Further, pilgrims can see first hand the surroundings in which Rasūlullāh ﷺ lived and delivered the message of Islām to the world.

Witnessing the massive assembly at 'Arafāt reminds the pilgrims of the Day of Judgement, when all of humanity will again assemble on this ground. Throwing stones at the symbols of Shaiṭān reminds the pilgrim of the spiritual struggle he or she must wage against evil temptation and distraction. All these experiences bring the pilgrim to new spiritual heights.

Moral Enrichment

Ḥajj teaches many vital moral lessons. Leaving family, friends, and social position behind, the pilgrim stands alone before Allāh ﷻ, repenting his sins and praying for guidance. Dressed in simple pieces of white cloth, the prince and the poor man stand equally before Allāh ﷻ, inspiring a feeling of humility in every pilgrim.

Ḥajj is also a trial of discipline and patience. In a crowd of thousands, the pilgrim suffers from heat, thirst, and exhaustion. Yet, the *Ḥajj* Code of Conduct requires him to control his anger and respond with kindness and brotherhood. The patience by which to bear such difficulties is a gift from Allāh ﷻ to the pilgrim.

Understanding the Purposes of Ḥajj

If someone intends to do *Ḥajj*, it is important that he understand the process, what it entails, why he is going to do it, and how he is to behave as a pilgrim. Ignorance of these things can prevent him from fully benefitting from the *Ḥajj* experience. Moreover, he may inadvertently ruin his *Ḥajj*.

The Right Intention of Ḥajj

The reward for *Ḥajj* depends on the sincerity of the pilgrim's intention. If one is going to *Ḥajj* for the sake of Allāh ﷻ, he will receive the full benefit and reward for it. If one is going to *Ḥajj* merely to earn the title of "*Al-Ḥājj,*" he may be sacrificing the sanctity of his *Ḥajj* before Allāh ﷻ. It is important for the pilgrim to have his priorities in order before making the intention to perform *Ḥajj*.

Rasūlullāh ﷺ said:

O people! Behold, the action(s) are but (judged) by intention,
and every one shall have but that what one intends for.
(Agreed upon)

✔ EXERCISES

1. How does the gathering of Muslims for *Ḥajj* each year benefit the *'Ummah* at large?
2. Which prophets are connected with the building of the Ka`bah?
3. How can pilgrims gain stronger faith from the experience of *Ḥajj*?
4. Describe two ways in which pilgrims can gain moral benefits from *Ḥajj*.
5. Give examples of how ignorance could ruin someone's *Ḥajj* or make him lose its full benefits.
6. If a Muslim goes for *Ḥajj* as an act of obedience to Allāh ﷻ, he will be rewarded by Allāh ﷻ accordingly. What about a Muslim who goes for *Ḥajj* only for the prestige and honor he will receive?

LESSON 47

SHARĪ 'AH: THE WAY OF JUSTICE

Sharī'ah includes all the fundamental laws that serve to guide human behavior as dictated by Allāh ﷻ. We have learned that a Muslim's purpose in this life is to earn the pleasure of Allāh ﷻ. By maintaining good behavior and avoiding evil, one strives for a successful *Ākhirah,* or life after death. The *Sharī'ah* is an essential tool in this pursuit, defining guidelines for good versus bad behavior over a wide range of situations. It also provides practical solutions to specific problems faced by Muslims on a daily basis. In essence, the *Sharī'ah* is a complete system of divine justice for Muslim life.

The Basis of the Sharī`ah

The *Sharī'ah* is based on the injunctions and laws laid down by Allāh ﷻ in the Qur'ān, as explained and demonstrated by Rasūlullāh ﷺ in his lifetime and recorded in the *Ḥadīth*. They are Allāh's eternal laws for mankind.

Can the Sharī`ah be Changed?

The basic laws of the *Sharī'ah* found in the Qur'ān do not change. They stand the test of time, because the nature of man and his basic needs do not change. No one is more aware of the needs of mankind than The Creator and Sustainer of mankind.

However, with the passage of time, certain circumstances may arise, and the Muslim *'Ummah* is expected to interpret the *Sharī'ah* under the guidance of its learned scholars, so that it will continue to uphold justice for every age and place.

The Sharī'ah Law Court

Certain aspects of the *Sharī 'ah* may be dealt with by the *Sharī'ah* courts. For example, if a person is accused of a crime, such as stealing or murder, the case should be presented to a judge who is learned in *Sharī 'ah*. If the person is found guilty, he should be punished in accordance with *Sharī 'ah*.

Matters relating to criminal acts, disputes, divorce, inheritance, and other family affairs can also be handled by the *Sharī'ah* courts.

A Muslim's Duty to Follow the Sharī'ah

Following the *Sharī 'ah* faithfully is the duty of every Muslim. Denying the *Sharī 'ah* is an act of direct disobedience to Allāh ﷻ. By defining limits of our behavior, these laws are meant to make our lives easier and more fulfilling, while preparing us for our ultimate destiny on the Day of Judgement. Thus, although to follow the *Sharī 'ah* is a duty, to do so benefits the welfare of all humankind.

Sharī'ah may be applied to all aspects of life, including relationships with family, friends, other Muslims, and even non-Muslims. For example, any dispute between individuals should be settled in accordance with the *Sharī'ah*, either by private agreement or through a *Sharī 'ah* court. Allāh ﷻ tells us in the Qur'ān to follow the commands of to Allāh ﷻ and *Sunnah* of Rasūlullāh ﷺ (that is, consult the Qur'ān and *Ḥadīth*).

وَمَآ ءَاتَىٰكُمُ ٱلرَّسُولُ فَخُذُوهُ وَمَا
نَهَىٰكُمْ عَنْهُ فَٱنتَهُوا۟ ۚ

Whatever the messenger gives you take it; and whatever he forbids you refrain from it.
(*Al-Hashr* 59:7)

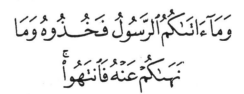

In addition, Allāh ﷻ has laid down laws defining the roles of husband, wife, mother, father, child, sibling, teacher, and student, etc., so that we can understand how to interact with each other in all situations.

It is important that we acknowledge the *Sharī'ah* to be the Supreme Law, unlike man-made laws that change with the fashions of the time. This point is made clear in the Qur'ān, which says:

وَمَن لَّمْ يَحْكُم
بِمَآ أَنزَلَ ٱللَّهُ فَأُو۟لَـٰٓئِكَ هُمُ ٱلْكَـٰفِرُونَ ﴿٤٤﴾

They who do not judge in accordance with what Allāh
has revealed are, indeed, deniers of the truth.
(*Al-Mā'idah* 5: 44)

✔ EXERCISES

1. What is the *Sharī 'ah*?
2. On what principle is the *Sharī'ah* based?
3. Can the basic laws of the *Sharī'ah* be changed? Why or why not?
4. What are the functions of the *Sharī'ah* law courts?
5. How should a dispute between two Muslims be settled?
6. Why should every Muslim try to live in accordance with the *Sharī'ah*?

LESSON 48

ISLĀMIC PRINCIPLES OF BUSINESS TRADE UNDER THE SHARĪ ‘AH

Fair Trade

The laws of *Sharī ‘ah* provide guidance for all aspects of life. The fields of business, commerce, and economics are especially addressed in Islāmic law.

The Qur’ān and *Ḥadīth* have given severe warnings about cheating in trade. Traders may cheat their customers in many ways: they may give a lesser measure or lesser weight than agreed upon; they may deceive the buyer about the quality of the product being sold; or they may hoard goods to create shortages and then raise the price due to high demand. All such practices have been forbidden in the Qur’ān and *Ḥadīth*.

Allāh ﷻ warns us in the Qur’ān:

أَوْفُوا الْكَيْلَ وَلَا
تَكُونُوا مِنَ الْمُخْسِرِينَ ﴿١٨١﴾ وَزِنُوا بِالْقِسْطَاسِ الْمُسْتَقِيمِ ﴿١٨٢﴾
وَلَا تَبْخَسُوا النَّاسَ أَشْيَاءَهُمْ وَلَا تَعْثَوْا فِي الْأَرْضِ مُفْسِدِينَ ﴿١٨٣﴾

Give full measure, and do not be of those who give less than (due). And weigh with a straight balance and do not wrong mankind in their goods, and do not do evil, making mischief in the earth.
(*Ash-Shu‘arā’* 26:181-3)

Rasūlullāh ﷺ also said:

He who holds a monopoly is a sinner.
(Transmitted by Muslim)

In a Muslim government, officials should be appointed to regulate business practices, so that such cheating and bad trading practices are controlled.

Prohibition of Ribā: Interest

The practice of giving or taking interest (*Ribā*) is strictly forbidden by Allāh ﷻ and His prophet. Such practices are one of the main causes of inflation (i.e. prices rising at a rate higher than the rate of the value of currency) and cripple the economy. In addition, sometimes people are forced into bankruptcy due to exorbitant interest rates. Muslims are warned not to make money an item of trade. They should instead establish Islāmic banks where money can be invested, borrowed and loaned in a *Ḥalāl* (lawful) manner, without giving or taking interest.

The Qur'ān says about interest:

يَٰٓأَيُّهَا ٱلَّذِينَ
ءَامَنُوا۟ لَا تَأْكُلُوا۟ ٱلرِّبَوٰٓا۟ أَضْعَٰفًا مُّضَٰعَفَةً ۖ وَٱتَّقُوا۟ ٱللَّهَ
لَعَلَّكُمْ تُفْلِحُونَ ١٣٠

O you who believe! Do not take Ribā, doubled and multiplied, but fear Allāh, so that you may prosper.
(*Āl-'Imrān* 3:130)

Prompt Payment of Debts

A Muslim who incurs a debt should settle it as soon as possible. Rasūlullāh ﷺ said:

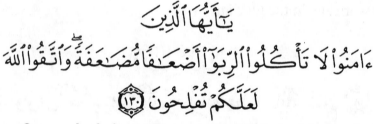

Delaying (payment of a debt) by a rich man is wrong-doing.
(Agreed Upon)

Prompt Payment to Workers

It is wrong to make a worker wait for earned wages. A *Ḥadīth* of Rasūlullāh ﷺ says:

Give the laborer his wages before his sweat dries.
(Transmitted by Ibn Mājah)

A Trustworthy Trader

The above Islāmic trade practices ensure that trade and business are conducted with good will, trust and benefit to the whole community.

Rasūlullāh ﷺ said in another *Ḥadīth*:

A trustworthy and truthful trader (or businessman) shall be with Rasūlullāh ﷺ and the truthful and the martyrs and the righteous (on the Day of Judgement)
(Transmitted by Tirmidhī)

✔ EXERCISES

1. Give some examples of trade practices forbidden by Islām.
2. What is hoarding?
3. What is *Ribā*?
4. How can Muslims avoid giving or taking *Ribā*?
5. What did Rasūlullāh ﷺ say about payment of debts?
6. What did Rasūlullāh ﷺ say about payment to laborers?

LESSON 49

MARRIAGE

As an individual matures, he goes through many changes. As an adult, he begins to desire companionship and a family of his own. The Islāmic manner of fulfilling this desire is through marriage. Marriage is strongly recommended in Islām for reasons well-documented in the Qur'ān and *Ḥadīth*. Let us discuss a few of them here.

Companionship

Allāh ﷻ says in the Qur'ān:

وَمِنْ ءَايَٰتِهِۦٓ أَنْ خَلَقَ لَكُم مِّنْ أَنفُسِكُمْ
أَزْوَٰجًا لِّتَسْكُنُوٓا۟ إِلَيْهَا وَجَعَلَ بَيْنَكُم مَّوَدَّةً وَرَحْمَةً ۚ
إِنَّ فِى ذَٰلِكَ لَءَايَٰتٍ لِّقَوْمٍ يَتَفَكَّرُونَ ﴿٢١﴾

And among His signs is this: that He created for you mates from among yourselves, so that you may dwell with them in tranquility; and He has put love and mercy between you. Truly, in that are Signs for people who think.
(*Ar-Rūm* 30:21)

The relationship between a husband and wife is naturally one of companionship; one that provides love, understanding, and care for both partners. These feelings come instinctively as guidance from Allāh ﷻ. This is how He blesses the union of husband and wife.

Protection from Shaiṭān's Temptations

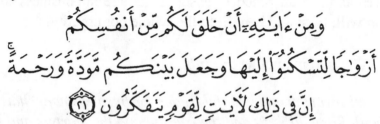

Upon maturity, men and women experience attraction toward each other. In marriage, these feelings are blessed by Allāh ﷻ. However, out of wedlock, to act on such feelings is forbidden, an act of *Ḥarām*. Rasūlullāh ﷺ warned:

Whenever a man is alone with a woman, Shaiṭān makes the third.
(Transmitted by Tirmidhī)

The Shaiṭān is always looking for opportunities to mislead us, so we must try to avoid circumstances that may create temptations beyond our control.

Through marriage, men and women can fulfill their attraction towards the opposite sex in a beautiful, Islāmic way; thus protecting them from temptation to commit adultery. Allāh ﷻ says in the Qur'ān that a husband and wife are "garments for one another." This means that they help protect each other from indecency, just as garments (clothes) cover and protect the body from nakedness.

Care of Children

Families form the foundation of the Muslim *'Ummah.* Islām encourages marriage to ensure the sanctity of the family and the proper upbringing of children.

A good marriage provides the basis for a healthy home environment, so children can get the best start in life. Children learn to love and care for others from their parents. Parents teach them the importance of proper manners, discipline, and honesty. They teach them to know their religion and to worship Allāh ﷻ. They guide them in their activities, until they are old enough to look after themselves.

How Marriage is Arranged

The western tradition of dating is forbidden in Islām. This is to protect individuals from situations in which they may be tempted by the *Shaiṭān.*

Therefore, marriage is usually arranged by parents, family members or friends.

Marriage may be arranged in several ways. For example, the parents of a boy or girl may look for a suitable partner for their daughter or son, or the boy may tell his parents that he wishes to marry a particular girl he knows. If the families, the boy and the girl all approve of the match, the marriage may be arranged.

How the Marriage Ceremony is Performed

There are many cultural customs associated with marriage. However, there are only four Islāmic requirements for marriage:

1. The ***Walī***. As guardian of the bride, this is the man who speaks on behalf of the girl's family and gives her in marriage. The *Wali* may be the girl's father or any other man appointed by the bride's family.
2. The giving of ***Ṣadaq (or Mihr)***, a gift to the bride from the bridegroom. It may be money or any other kind of gift. It may be of any value as long as it is acceptable to the bride.
3. ***Witnesses***. The marriage must be witnessed by at least two very reliable male witnesses.
4. ***Sigah***. This is the formal process in which the bridegroom or his representative asks for the bride's hand in marriage, and the bride's *Walī* agrees to give the bride, who is then formally accepted.

Rasūlullāh ﷺ also strongly recommended that a wedding should be publicized.

Responsibilities in Marriage

The husband and wife are to be faithful to each other in marriage. With love, care, and understanding, they should try to satisfy each other to the best of their ability.

The husband is legally responsible for supporting his wife and children, providing their housing, clothing and food, according to his ability. Even if the wife is wealthy or is earning money, the husband is still responsible for the maintenance of his family. However, she may help him if she wishes.

The wife should respect her husband as head of the family. He should consult her, and she may offer him advice, but final decisions on matters affecting the family should be left to the husband, as long as his decisions are not contrary to Islāmic teachings. In turn, the husband is expected to be kind and reasonable in his treatment of his wife. Many injunctions in the Qur'ān and *Ḥadīth* of Rasūlullāh ﷺ have emphasized the importance of a husband's just treatment of his wife.

One such *Ḥadīth* states:

The best among you is he who is kindest to his wife.
(Transmitted by Tirmidhi)

✔ EXERCISES

1. Name some of the benefits of marriage to the husband and wife.
2. How does marriage and family life benefit children?
3. What are the four requirements for a valid Islāmic marriage?
4. Name some of the duties of husband and wife towards each other.

LESSON 50

DIVORCE

Divorce is Hated.by Allāh ﷻ

Marriage is very important for a Muslim. The separation of husband and wife by divorce is a great misfortune, particularly if they have children. Rasūlullāh ﷺ said:

Of all the things which Allāh ﷻ has permitted,
the thing He most hates is divorce.
(Transmitted by Abū Dā'ūd)

Therefore, divorce is not to be considered an option unless all means of keeping the husband and wife together have failed. If husband and wife cannot live together in peace, Allāh ﷻ does not force them to stay married. Nevertheless, divorce should be considered a last resort.

Three Categories of Divorce

There are three main categories of divorce:

1. Divorce by the husband
2. *Khul`ah:* divorce at the request of the wife
3. Divorce pronounced by a *Sharī`ah* Court

CASE 1: ***Divorce by the Husband***

The proper way for a husband to give a divorce is to declare his intention once, when the wife is free from menstruation. This is a revocable divorce.

The wife should pass the time of her *'Iddah* or waiting period (about three months) in her husband's house, and he should provide her food, clothing, and other necessities as usual. It is hoped that the husband and wife will reconcile during this waiting period. If this happens, the husband may revoke the divorce, and the marriage is reinstated. Divorce can be revoked in this way twice, but on the third occasion it cannot be revoked.

If the *'Iddah* period is completed, and the couple is unable to reconcile, the divorce becomes permanent. Both parties are then free to marry other people. However, once divorced, the same couple cannot remarry each other unless the woman first marries someone else. It means the couple could only get married if the woman marries some one and is either divorced or her husband dies.

In case of divorce by the husband, he has no right to take back any of the dowry or presents he has given his wife.

CASE 2: ***Divorce at the Request of the Wife (Khul`ah)***

A wife who wishes to be released from marriage may ask her husband to give her *Khul`ah*. In this case, she agrees to give back all or part of her dowry, and anything else that is mutually agreed upon in return for her release.

CASE 3: ***Divorce pronounced by a Sharī'ah Court or Court of Law***

If her husband is not treating her properly, a wife may take her complaint to the court. The court will investigate her complaint, and if it is found to be valid, the judge may order the marriage to be dissolved. In this case, the wife is not required to return anything to the husband.

The 'Iddah

The *'Iddah*, or waiting period of the wife, has two main purposes. The first is to allow time for reconciliation. The second is to establish whether the divorced wife is pregnant. *'Iddah* covers three clear intervals between menstrual periods, normally lasting between three to four months. If the divorced wife is pregnant, *'Iddah* lasts until she delivers her child.

Custody of Children

In the case of divorce, children should normally go with their mother, boys until puberty and girls until their marriage. If the mother gets married again, or for some reason, is unable to look after the children, they should go to her own mother, or her grandmother, or her sister. If none of these relatives of the mother can look after them, they should go to the husband's mother or his grandmother. If they cannot look after them, the children should stay with their father. These are the rules for custody of children in the Mālikī School of *Sharī'ah* (Islāmic Law). However, wherever the children stay, their father is responsible for their sustenance (cost of feeding, clothing, education, etc.)

✔ EXERCISES

1. Quote one *Ḥadīth* about divorce.
2. What are the three main types of divorce?
3. What is the *'Iddah*?
4. Who is responsible for providing a divorced wife's food, clothes, and accommodations during her *'Iddah*?
5. What is the order of priority among relatives for custody of children after divorce?

IQRA'
TRANSLITERATION CHART

q	ق	*	z	ز		'	أ ء	*
k	ك		s	س		b	ب	
l	ل		sh	ش		t	ت	
m	م		ṣ	ص	*	th	ث	*
n	ن		ḍ	ض	*	j	ج	
h	هـ		ṭ	ط	*	ḥ	ح	*
w	و		ẓ	ظ	*	kh	خ	*
y	ي		ʻ	ع	*	d	د	
			gh	غ	*	dh	ذ	*
			f	ف		r	ر	

SHORT VOWELS	LONG VOWELS	DIPHTHONGS
a \ ـَ	ā \ ـا	aw \ ـَوْ
u \ ـُ	ū \ ـُو	ai \ ـَيْ
i \ ـِ	ī \ ـِي	
Such as: *kataba* كَتَبَ	Such as: *Kitāb* كتاب	Such as: *Lawh* لَوْح
Such as: *Qul* قُلْ	Such as: *Mamnūn* مَمْنُون	Such as: *'Ain* عَيْن
Such as: *Ni'mah* نِعْمَة	Such as: *Dīn* دين	

* Special attention should be given to the symbols marked with stars for they have no equivalent in the English sounds .

Note : Letters in parenthesis (a),(i),(u) appear in writing but are not pronounced.

ISLAMIC INVOCATIONS:

Rasūlullāh, *Ṣalla Allahu 'alaihi wa Sallam* (صَلَّى اللّٰهُ عَلَيْهِ وَسَلَّمَ), and the Qur'ān teaches us to glorify Allāh ﷻ when we mention His Name and to invoke His Blessings when we mention the names of His Angels, Messengers, the *Ṣaḥābah* and the Pious Ancestors.

When we mention the Name of Allāh we must say: *Subḥāna-hū Wa-Ta'ālā* (سُبْحَانَهُ وَتَعَالَى), Glorified is He and High. In this book we write ﷻ to remind ourselves to glorify Allāh.

When we mention the name of Rasūlullāh ﷺ we must say: *Ṣalla Allāhu 'alai-hi wa-Sallam,* (صَلَّى اللّٰهُ عَلَيْهِ وَسَلَّمَ), May Allāh's Blessings and Peace be upon him.
We write ﷺ to remind ourselves to invoke Allāh's Blessings on Rasūlullāh.

When we mention the name of an angel or a prophet we must say: *Alai-hi-(a)s-Salām* (عَلَيْهِ السَّلَامُ), Upon him be peace.
We write ؑ to remind ourselves to invoke Allāh's Peace upon him.

When we hear the name of the *Ṣaḥābah* we must say:
For a *Ṣaḥābī, Raḍiya-(A)llāhu Ta'ālā 'an-hu* (رَضِيَ اللّٰهُ تَعَالَى عَنْهُ), May Allāh be pleased with him.
We write ؓ to remind ourselves to invoke Allah's pleasure on them.

For more than two, *Raḍiya-(A)llāhu Ta'ālā 'an-hum,* (رَضِيَ اللّٰهُ تَعَالَى عَنْهُمْ), May Allāh be pleased with them.
We write ؓ to remind ourselves to invoke Allah's pleasure on them.

For a *Ṣaḥābiyyah, Raḍiya-(A)llāhu Ta'ālā 'an-hā* (رَضِيَ اللّٰهُ تَعَالَى عَنْهَا), May Allāh be pleased with her.
We write ؓ to remind ourselves to invoke Allah's pleasure on her.

For two of them, *Raḍiya-(A)llāhu Ta'ālā 'an-humā* (رَضِيَ اللّٰهُ تَعَالَى عَنْهُمَا), May Allāh be pleased with both of them.
We write ؓ to remind ourselves to invoke Allah's pleasure on them.

When we hear the name of the Pious Ancestor *(As-Salaf aṣ-Ṣāliḥ)* we must say:
For a man, *Raḥmatu-(A)llāh 'alai-hi*(رَحْمَةُ اللّٰهِ عَلَيْهِ), May Allāh's Mercy be upon him.
For a woman, *Raḥmatu-(A)llāh 'alai-hā* (رَحْمَةُ اللّٰهِ عَلَيْهَا), May Allāh's Mercy be with her.